IRAN AND
THE FORMER
SOVIET SOUTH

The Former Soviet South project is sponsored by:

- A. Meredith Jones & Co. Ltd
- B.A.T Industries plc
- The British Petroleum Company plc
- ENI S.p.A.
- John Laing International Limited
- Statoil

Series editor: Edmund Herzig

FORMER SOVIET SOUTH PROJECT

IRAN AND THE FORMER SOVIET SOUTH

Edmund Herzig

THE ROYAL INSTITUTE OF
INTERNATIONAL AFFAIRS
Russian and CIS Programme

CONTENTS

SUMMARY

The break-up of the Soviet Union confronted Iran with a set of challenges and opportunities. On the one hand the long-standing threat presented by the USSR receded and the door opened for much closer contact with Central Asia and the Transcaucasus, now divided among eight new independent states, six of them with at least nominally Muslim majority populations. On the other the USA, Iran's foremost ideological foe, was no longer balanced by a Soviet superpower and there were dangers for Iran's security from the volatility and instability of the new states. How should this sudden and unforeseen situation be handled? Should the Islamic Republic of Iran exploit the weakness of the new states to export radical Islamic ideology and stamp its authority as a major regional power, or should it follow a more neighbourly and cooperative path? Not only the new states, but also Moscow and the West, watched Tehran's moves with close attention.

In this paper it is argued that pragmatic interests – reducing Iran's international isolation, opening avenues for economic cooperation and commercial exchange, restoring religious and cultural links, and safeguarding the mutually advantageous relationship with Russia – have consistently been given a higher priority than ideology in Iran's relations with the former Soviet South. The basis for steadily expanding political, economic and cultural relations with all of the new states has now been established. The future direction of relations will be determined by political and economic developments in Iran, in the former Soviet South and in Russia.

ABOUT THE AUTHOR

Edmund Herzig is a senior research fellow coordinating the Former Soviet South Project of the Russian and CIS Programme of the Royal Institute of International Affairs. He is currently on leave from Manchester University, where he is a lecturer in the Department of Middle Eastern Studies and a member of the Research Group on Central Asia and the Caucasus. He is a specialist on the history of Iran and the Transcaucasus, as well as on contemporary Armenia.

ACKNOWLEDGMENTS

I would like to thank all the participants in a study group at the Royal Institute of International Affairs on 23 June 1995, when a preliminary draft of this paper was discussed; I have benefited greatly from their comments and criticisms. Nilufar Fatemi, Tamara Dragadze and Roy Allison also suggested improvements to the draft. I am indebted to Morteza Aboutalebi and Mehrdad Mohsenin of the Institute for Political and International Studies (Tehran) and to Tony Hyman, who all kindly provided issues of the *Majalleh-ye motale'at-e Asiya-ye Markazi va Qafqaz* (*Central Asia and Caucasus Review*). The staff of the Royal Institute of International Affairs Library assisted with sources and references. Special thanks are due to Gudrun Persson, who carried out a major part of the research for the paper using the Foreign Broadcast Information Service *Daily Reports* and other sources.

June 1995   E.H.

ABBREVIATIONS

CSCE	Conference on Security and Cooperation in Europe (now OSCE – Organization for Security and Cooperation in Europe)
ECO	Economic Cooperation Organization
FBIS	Foreign Broadcast Information Service, *Daily Report*
FSS	Former Soviet South
FSU	Former Soviet Union
GCC	Gulf Cooperation Council
MMAMQ	*Majalleh-ye motale'at-e Asiya-ye Markazi va Qafqaz (Central Asia and Caucasus Review)*
OIC	Organization of the Islamic Conference
SWB	BBC, *Summary of World Broadcasts*

Map 1: Iran and the former Soviet South

Map 2: Iran – railways

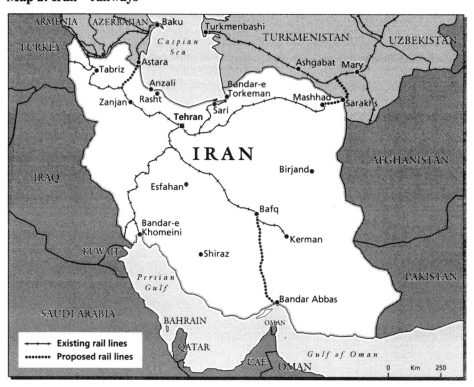

1 INTRODUCTION

The collapse of the Soviet Union and the emergence of new independent post-Soviet states has affected Iran profoundly. Iran shared a 2,250-kilometre frontier with the USSR, but now across its northern land border it faces independent Armenia, Azerbaijan and Turkmenistan, and from its northern coast can reach out across the Caspian Sea to four new littoral states: Azerbaijan, the Russian Federation, Kazakhstan and Turkmenistan. Such fundamental changes so close at hand present important challenges and opportunities, and in Iran, as elsewhere, there has been considerable debate about the nature and implications of these changes and how best to respond to them.[1] While the debate continues, the government, certain sectors of the economy and to a lesser extent wider society have started to develop links with the states and peoples of the former Soviet Union (FSU). This study explores Iranian perceptions of the changes taking place across the country's northern borders, traces the development of relations with the eight new Central Asian and Transcaucasian states of the former Soviet South (FSS), and considers the key determinants that are likely to shape Iranian interests and involvement in coming years.

New hopes, new fears

For the past two centuries the greatest threat to the security and territorial integrity of Iran has been posed by the Russian empire and its successor the Soviet Union. In the early nineteenth century Russia took from Iran the Transcaucasian territories that Iranian dynasties had claimed since the sixteenth and seventeenth centuries, when the territorial shape of the modern Iranian state was first established by the Safavi kings. In the twentieth century, the Soviet-supported nationalist-revolutionary and separatist movements in Gilan, Kurdistan and Azerbaijan after the two world wars posed argu-

---

[1] In addition to numerous articles on Central Asia and the Caucasus in Iranian newspapers and journals, the Foreign Ministry Institute for Political and International Studies has established a Center of Central Asia and Caucasia Research, which has organized a number of conferences and publishes a journal: *Majalleh-ye motale'at-e Asiya-ye Markazi va Qafqaz (The Central Asia and Caucasus Review)* (hereafter *MMAMQ*).

ably the greatest challenges to Iran's territorial integrity until the Iraqi invasion of 1980. For most of this period Russian power had to some extent been balanced by the presence of a second great power in the Middle East – first Britain and, after the Second World War, the USA. If the Western powers did not present the same continuous direct military threat as Russia, they both obstructed Iran's territorial and security ambitions in the Persian Gulf, and Britain occupied Iranian territory on several occasions (most notably in conjunction with its Russian and Soviet ally in both world wars, and in spite of Iranian declarations of neutrality). The alternation of great-power rivalry and collaboration has exerted a strong influence over Iranian history since the early nineteenth century, not only forming the context in which Iran's foreign policy took shape, but also profoundly affecting the country's internal economic and political development, in areas as diverse as railway construction, constitutional reform and, of course, the oil industry. In Iranian popular belief great-power politics not only affected, but determined, the course of modern Iranian history, which is itself viewed as a period of political and military weakness, economic subservience and cultural decline unprecedented in the annals of a powerful nation and a great civilization. The sinister machinations of Russia, Britain and the USA are commonly blamed for all Iran's ills, from the failure of the Constitutional Revolution and the Mosaddeq government to the country's belated and uneven socio-economic development. Reaction against the great powers and the assertion of independence and distinct values and identity were among the most potent forces in the 1979 Revolution and gave rise to its most powerful slogans: 'Neither East nor West, but an Islamic republic!'

Against this background it is clear that the break-up of the Soviet Union was an event of great significance for Iran, one that in many ways was advantageous to the Islamic Republic. On the ideological level it demonstrated that the existing world order was not immutable and that even the greatest powers were vulnerable. The sudden collapse of communism throughout Eastern Europe and the Soviet Union was seen as a victory for faith and spirituality over atheism and materialism. In terms of security it removed, to a safer distance if not altogether, the threat of Russian armies and partially redressed the long-standing asymmetry in Iran's relations with its northern neighbour. Still weak relative to Russia, Iran now appears a powerful force in comparison with the new Central Asian and Transcaucasian states. Apart from the negative benefits arising from the removal of a major military and ideological threat, the disintegration of the USSR and the opening of the borders offered many new opportunities. The Iranian government could now hope to develop political and even security relations with the new states, enhancing its regional status and reducing its international isolation. The opening up of economic relations and the development of Iranian infrastructure to link the FSS to world markets promised a much-needed boost for the Iranian economy. Finally there was the possibility of restoring ties with peoples who had much in common with the Iranians in terms of shared history, religion, culture and language.

The new situation also held dangers, however, which soon made themselves felt. The end of the bipolar world order left the USA stronger and less constrained than before. This in itself constituted a threat to the Islamic Republic, for although in the 1980s relations with the Soviet Union had often been bad,[2] America was always the Great Satan. Relations with the USA have, if anything, deteriorated further in the 1990s, in part because, with the communist enemy defeated, militant Islamic states are now viewed in Washington as the greatest threat to America's interests and Western values. There are clear indications that the US government intends to increase pressure on Iran through the policy of 'dual containment' and will actively oppose Iranian engagement in the FSS. For Iran, any reduction in the Soviet-Russian threat has, therefore, been counterbalanced by a corresponding increase in that posed by the USA. On a regional level, the gains in security accruing from the removal of the Soviet military threat from Iran's northern borders are offset by the dangers arising from regional instability and conflict. War and extreme political instability in Azerbaijan, Georgia and Tajikistan and outbreaks of inter-ethnic violence elsewhere in the region leave the Iranian government anxious about the domestic impact of these conflicts and fearing their spread or escalation, as well as the possibility of outside interference and of new refugee crises – all of which are familiar from its experiences with Afghanistan and Iraq. Now, more than ever, Iran sees itself surrounded by conflict and instability. A further potential threat is posed by the upsurge in nationalist sentiment among the Turkic peoples of the FSU, which might have an impact among Iran's minorities, and particularly by the creation of the independent nation-states of Azerbaijan and Turkmenistan, which might claim the loyalties of Iran's significant Azerbaijani and Turkmen populations.

The following chapters will examine the development of Iran's political, economic and cultural-religious relations with the new Central Asian and Transcaucasian states in the light of these opportunities and challenges. First, however, two further questions must be touched on: (1) the broader foreign and regional policy context in which Iran's approach to the FSS is framed; and (2) the issue of Iran's relations with Russia, which falls outside the scope of this study, but which to a great extent overshadows and defines relations with other states of the former Soviet Union.

[2] See A.Y. Yodfat, *The Soviet Union and Revolutionary Iran* (New York: St Martin's Press, 1984); M. Varasteh, 'The Soviet Union and Iran, 1979–89', in A. Ehteshami and M. Varasteh (eds), *Iran and the International Community* (London and New York: Routledge, 1991), pp. 46–59; R. Herrmann, 'The Role of Iran in Soviet Perceptions and Policy, 1946–88' and R.O. Freedman, 'Gorbachev, Iran, and the Iran–Iraq War', in N.R. Keddie and M.J. Gasiorowski (eds), *Neither East nor West: Iran, the Soviet Union, and the United States* (New Haven and London: Yale University Press, 1990), pp. 63–99 and 115–41.

Iranian foreign and security policy

A combination of strategic location and energy resources has made Iran a focus for great power interest and competition throughout the modern period. This fact has profoundly affected Iranians' perceptions of the world, of the historical process and international relations.[3] All Iranian governments, whatever their political orientation, have developed their foreign policy against this background, and have tried to develop strategies accordingly. In essence the aim has been to balance the great powers in a way that best serves the interests of Iran, by allowing it to defend its sovereignty and integrity against their ambitions and intrigues. Various approaches have been adopted, with varying degrees of success: these include positive equilibrium (offering something to both powers); negative equilibrium (refusing concessions to either power); third-power strategy (encouraging the involvement of another Western power, such as Germany, to offset the great powers' influence); alliance with one or other power. The end of the bipolar world of the Cold War era has profoundly altered the global balance of power and with it Iran's foreign policy objectives and alternatives. In the mid-1990s Iran is no longer faced with the problem of balancing two great powers; rather it needs to develop strategies to cope with a dominant and unfriendly USA. In addition (but not coincidentally in Iranian thinking) there are security concerns stemming from regional instability and militarization, as well as the country's serious unresolved economic problems.[4]

The post-Khomeini leadership's response to this challenge has been a combination of initiatives, not all readily compatible. In the first place, the Iranian government has made considerable efforts to reduce its international isolation by convincing other states that Iran is a 'normal' state, committed to upholding international law and maintaining the norms of international conduct, a potential partner rather than a threat. Progress in this direction has been slow and uneven – particularly in important areas such as the Persian Gulf and Europe[5] – largely because of inconsistencies in policy and behaviour, and continuing differences within the leadership and between the various agencies involved in Iran's foreign relations. The lack of international support for

---

[3] G. Fuller, *The Center of the Universe: the Geopolitics of Iran* (Boulder, CO: Westview Press, 1990), pp. 17–23, 241–6; S.T. Hunter, *Iran and the World: Continuity in a Revolutionary Decade* (Bloomington, IN: Indiana University Press, 1990), pp. 37–45.

[4] For recent analyses of Iran's foreign policy, see M. Mandelbaum (ed.), *Central Asia and the World* (New York: Council on Foreign Relations Press, 1994), pp. 393–412; A. Tarrock, 'Iran's Foreign Policy since the Gulf War', *Australian Journal of International Affairs*, vol. 48, no. 2 (1994), pp. 267–80; J. Calabrese, *Revolutionary Horizons: Regional Foreign Policy in Post-Khomeini Iran* (Basingstoke: Macmillan, 1994); K.L. Afrasiabi, *After Khomeini: New Directions in Iran's Foreign Policy* (Boulder, CO: Westview Press, 1994).

[5] Calabrese, op. cit., pp. 45–74; F. Halliday, 'An Elusive Normalization: Western Europe and the Iranian Revolution', *Middle East Journal*, vol. 48, no. 2 (1994), pp. 309–26.

4

the US sanctions against Iran announced in May 1995 indicates, however, that Iran's efforts have not been wasted. In addition to cultivating bilateral links, Iran has also endeavoured to improve its image and work more effectively through a variety of multilateral and regional organizations, such as the Economic Cooperation Organization (ECO), and the Organization of Islamic Conference (OIC). Uniting the Muslim and other oppressed peoples against great-power domination was always an important part of revolutionary Iran's international mission, but the special emphasis on regional cooperation and multilateralism is a distinctive feature of current Iranian foreign policy. Specific economic, security or ideological objectives may be more readily attainable through cooperation than through individual efforts, but in addition the process of participation itself serves Iran's interests by contributing to its reintegration into the international community. Moreover, association with other states in regional and multilateral groupings helps offset Iran's weakness relative to the USA. In this respect the long-standing tradition of counterbalancing a threatening great power continues, in revised form, to occupy a place in Iran's foreign policy; if there is no single contemporary state capable of balancing the USA, Iran hopes to achieve the same end through groups of states.

National security is a major concern in Iran's foreign and especially regional relations. Perceptions and objectives still bear the deep imprint of the experience of the Iran–Iraq war.[6] The country's military rebuilding concentrates on developing the capacity for defence against invasion, aerial or missile attack. Security policy emphasizes self-reliance and domestic arms production as well as diversification of arms procurement. The latter has formed an important element in Iran's relations with a number of former Warsaw Pact countries, as well as with China and North Korea. Perceived essential national security concerns are given primacy in relations with neighbouring states, as is shown by the use of force against Mojahedin-e Khalq and Kurdish bases in Iraq, by the insistence on the principle of territorial integrity *vis-à-vis* Iraq, and by the readiness to cooperate with neighbouring states on mutual non-interference in internal affairs. Iran has also attempted to build up regional security cooperation in an effort to contain the threat posed by regional conflicts and instability, to guard against any revival of Iraq, and to counterbalance US involvement in the region.[7] So far these attempts have achieved little success; in spite of a considerable improvement in bilateral relations since the end of the Iran–Iraq war, the Arab Gulf states continue to consider Iran a potential threat and to rely on the USA for their security.[8]

---

[6] On security policy see S. Chubin, *Iran's National Security Policy: Capabilities, Intentions and Impact* (Washington DC: The Carnegie Endowment for International Peace, 1994); Calabrese, op. cit., pp. 3–12, 34–43.
[7] Ramazani, op. cit., pp. 401–3.
[8] Calabrese, op. cit., pp. 45–74.

The post-Khomeini leadership has attached special significance to its economic policy, correctly viewing this as the crucial test of the government's competence and legitimacy in the eyes of most Iranians; for this reason economic relations now constitute an important foreign policy concern. No analyst doubts the severity of Iran's economic difficulties, arising from a combination of the costs of war reconstruction, bad policies (particularly in the first decade after the revolution), mismanagement and corruption, rapid population growth, low oil prices and obstacles to outside investment. Some economists, however, see the reforms of recent years – privatization, the shift to a market economy, the emphasis on non-oil exports, import substitution and smaller-scale and local projects – beginning to have a positive effect, while others remain pessimistic.[9] Foreign economic policy has concentrated on finding markets for Iran's non-oil exports, economic and technical cooperation (particularly with other Islamic and developing countries) and the creation of free trade zones. In foreign economic relations there is the same emphasis on regional cooperation and multilateral organizations – the attempt to revitalize ECO being the clearest example – as in political and security relations.[10]

In Western eyes the foreign policy of Iran since the revolution has generally been associated less with the kinds of interests outlined above and more with the export of radical Islam, support for a variety of high-profile Islamic causes and a preference for what is euphemistically referred to as unconventional diplomacy: the exploitation of propaganda, sedition and terrorism. Western officials, moreover, remain convinced that this aspect of Iran's foreign involvement is still very much alive in the Middle East and elsewhere. In the view of some specialists there is a clear dichotomy between this ideological, revolutionary, religious, 'irrational' urge and the rational pursuit of national interest in Iranian foreign policy. But while there can be no doubt that the Islamic Republic's ideological commitments often clash with Iran's national geopolitical and economic interests (e.g. in the Salman Rushdie affair and the relationship with the USA),[11] one can also identify areas where other interests (security versus economic interest; short-term versus long-term advantage) do not harmonize, for example in the Abu Musa and the Tunbs islands dispute with the United Arab Emirates.

It seems more useful to consider ideology as one among a number of factors shaping Iranian foreign policy, though one which for a variety of reasons is particularly

---

[9] H. Amirahmadi, *Revolution and Economic Transition: The Iranian Experience* (Albany, NY: SUNY, 1990). Recent relatively optimistic assessments are by V. Petrossian in *Middle East Economic Digest* (10 February 1995), pp. 8–15, and by N. Mamedova in *Aziya i Afrika segodnya*, 8–9 (1994), pp. 40–44. For a contrasting view, see K. Ehsani in *Middle East Report*, 191 (1994), pp. 16–21. Both Mamedova's and Ehsani's articles form part of longer features on Iran in the same issues.

[10] Calabrese, op. cit., pp. 29–34.

[11] Chubin, op. cit., pp. 12–13.

difficult to harmonize with others.[12] Halliday's analysis of Iran as a revolutionary state, and comparison with early Soviet foreign policy provide a useful approach for understanding this question.[13] There is another parallel to be drawn with the Soviet experience in the dialectics of Islam in Iranian foreign policy. Far from being invariably a focus for radical revolutionary appeal, Islam can have several values in Iranian foreign policy and is regularly cited to justify a range of positions and methods. In the mid-1990s Islam is drawn on as often to justify state-to-state cooperative relations (both in bilateral relations with Islamic countries such as Pakistan, and in the attempt to mobilize Islamic state blocs through organizations such as ECO and OIC), as to support radical causes (e.g. Palestine, Lebanon, Kashmir, Algeria). Iran uses Islam to bolster its international status not only as the leading radical Islamic state, but also as the homeland of Islamic Persian civilization, a great old-world civilization which ranks with those of India and China.[14]

This ramified conception of Islam, which has received relatively little attention from commentators and which tends to be obscured by the 'Islam versus national interest' approach to Iranian foreign policy, to some extent mediates between nationalism and internationalism, pragmatism and ideology, and gives the leadership room for manoeuvre in foreign policy, at least within the constraints imposed by internal politics (see below). In this respect it is noteworthy that in areas that touch most vitally on Iran's security and economic interests, it is the normative, cooperative, civilizational aspect of Islam that is emphasized, rather than the radical, confrontational, revolutionary element.

Finally, no discussion of Iranian foreign policy, however brief, would be complete without reference to internal politics. In this respect the crucial features are the continuing multiplicity of interests and agencies involved in the foreign policy process (despite the relative success of the post-Khomeini leadership in consolidating its position and controlling state and quasi-state institutions); divisions within the leadership on important foreign policy issues; the adoption of foreign policy positions to cement consensus within the leadership rather than on their merits as policy; and the revolutionary heritage, on which the government's legitimacy in its own eyes and among its committed supporters depends, yet which acts as a constraint in policy formulation. These factors, whose interaction and relative weight is often difficult to assess from outside, play an important role in setting the limits of innovation and development in Iranian foreign policy.[15] It is important, however, to emphasize that because this issue

---

[12] Afrasiabi, op. cit., pp. 9–19.

[13] Halliday, op. cit., p. 311.

[14] See, for example, A. Khorram, 'Joint Cooperation between China, India and Iran', *Iranian Journal of International Affairs*, vol. 7, no. 1 (1995), pp. 197–8.

[15] Afrasiabi, op. cit., pp. 19–36; Chubin, op. cit., pp. 65–73.

of policy towards the FSS only arose in about 1990 it is free of the revolutionary associations that continue to dominate other issues (such as relations with the USA). Moreover, because Iran's relations with this region were formed so late, the president, the National Security Council and the foreign ministry have been able to maintain control over Central Asian and Transcaucasian policy;[16] there is little evidence of involvement or even significant interest in relations with the FSS from other agencies with foreign policy interests dating from the early years of the revolution.

Relations with Russia

For Iran, as for the rest of the world, the question of relations with the Russian Federation overshadows other concerns in the FSU. Iran's vital interests are closely affected by what happens in the FSS, but they are still more closely affected by developments in Russia, which in any case exert a powerful influence on the nature and direction of change throughout the FSU. The general trend in relations between Tehran and Moscow has been positive since the end of the Iran–Iraq war and the Soviet withdrawal from Afghanistan. The decisive upturn in relations began with a remarkable letter from Ayatollah Khomeini to Mikhail Gorbachev in January 1989. In the early years of *glasnost* and *perestroika*, Khomeini had not been favourably impressed by the Soviet reforms and had tended to prefer the politburo conservatives, led by Igor Ligachev, to the reformers, but in this letter, delivered by a high-level personal delegation, he praised Mikhail Gorbachev for his reforms, but went on to argue that communism was dead. He urged him not to turn from the failed materialism of Marxism to the failing materialism of the West, but to retain his independence and find spiritual values through the study of Islam. With hindsight, the concluding paragraph sounds like Iran's opening salvo in the ideological battle for the soul of the Soviet Union (see below): 'the Islamic Republic of Iran, as the greatest and most powerful base of the Islamic world, can easily fill the ideological vacuum of your system'.[17] The letter was followed by a series of high-level contacts, notably a visit by the then speaker of parliament, Akbar Hashemi-Rafsanjani, soon after Khomeini's death. In the course of this visit agreements were reached on trade, Caspian oil exploration, the resumption of Iranian natural gas supplies, the construction of dams in Iran, defence and nuclear cooperation, and the linking of the Iranian and Soviet Central Asian railway systems. The time-

---

[16] S.K. Sajjadpour, 'Iran, the Caucasus and Central Asia', in A. Banuazizi and M. Weiner (eds), *The New Geopolitics of Central Asia and its Borderlands* (London and New York: I.B. Tauris, 1994), pp. 199–200.

[17] An English translation of the letter is given in *SWB* ME/0354 A/6, 10 January 1989. See also the comments of Akbar Hashemi-Rafsanjani (*SWB* ME/0359 A/5, 16 January 1989) and Ayatollah Khamene'i (cited in G. Fuller, op. cit., pp. 176–7).

scale of the agreements was fifteen years and their direct value $6 billion, although Iran estimated its overall spending on the projects would be $15 billion. During the same visit the two sides agreed not to interfere in each other's internal affairs – a sensitive issue for both sides, as placards of Khomeini were being displayed in demonstrations in Azerbaijan over the Mountainous (*Nagorny*) Karabagh issue, while Iran was already nervous about the possible impact of nationalist and irredentist sentiment in the Soviet South – and, in a startling gesture of ideological reconciliation, Akbar Hashemi-Rafsanjani was allowed to preach in Baku's main Shi'i mosque.[18]

Russia, which fully shares Western anxieties about the spread of Islamic fundamentalism, seems on the face of it an unlikely friend for Iran, but Soviet and Russian experience of the Islamic threat has been focused on the Afghan Mojahedin and their Pakistani and Saudi Arabian backers rather than on Iran's mullahs. Russia's leaders clearly believe (and experience seems to justify their belief) that any Iranian tendency towards Islamic militancy in the FSU can most effectively be discouraged through engagement. Russia sees Iran as a useful counterweight to American, Turkish and Turkic ascendancy in the region and also has an interest in access to Iran's Persian Gulf ports.[19]

For Iran the benefits of the relationship are manifold. Russia is an important trading partner, a major supplier of arms and a willing collaborator in technological, most notably nuclear, projects. Russia and Iran share similar anxieties about nationalism and irredentism in the FSS. Russia guards the external borders of the CIS (except in Azerbaijan), and Iran perceives its security interest in the maintenance and control of existing borders. Moreover, while Russia may no longer be the second superpower, it remains committed to keeping outsiders out of security structures in the CIS (except in the context of multi-national peace-keeping operations) and is the force most likely and able to check the further expansion of US interests and involvement in the wider region. Iran, like Russia, views Turkey's regional ambitions and the possible spread of some form of pan-Turkic ideology with suspicion.

Since 1989 there have been considerable strains on the Moscow–Tehran relationship: the Soviet army's bloody entry into Baku in January 1990, Russia's support for the ex-communists in the Tajik civil war, and the war in Chechenia in 1995. Each of these episodes tested Iran's commitment to the relationship with Russia against its support for Islamic causes and the liberation struggle of Muslim peoples in the FSU. In each case, and in the face of domestic pressure, Iran's leaders gave the higher

[18] *The Financial Times*, 21, 23, 25, 26 June 1989; *International Herald Tribune*, 3 July 1989. See also M. Mesbahi, 'Gorbachev's "New Thinking" and Islamic Iran: From Containment to Reconciliation', in H. Amirahmadi and N. Entessar (eds), *Reconstruction and Regional Diplomacy in the Persian Gulf* (London and New York: Routledge, 1992), pp. 260–96.
[19] D. Hearst in *The Guardian*, 31 May 1995.

priority to the relationship with Russia.[20] It may be an overstatement to talk, as some have done, of a new Moscow–Tehran axis (Baghdad and Erevan are also sometimes included in the putative alliance), but it is evident that the present governments in Russia and Iran have found the basis for a durable positive relationship.[21] An appreciation of this fact is essential for understanding Iran's perceived interests and policies in the FSS.

---

[20] G. Tett in *The Financial Times*, 27 January 1995.

[21] See the interviews with Akbar Hashemi-Rafsanjani and Vladimir Yurtaev in *Aziya i Afrika segodnya*, 8–9 (1994), pp. 38–9 and 45–8. Also of interest is the interview with Sergei Tretyakov on Irano–Russian nuclear cooperation, pp. 49–50.

2 IRAN'S POLITICAL AND SECURITY INTERESTS

The development of the international relations of the new Central Asian and Transcaucasian states has often been presented in terms of a competition for political and ideological influence. The notion that the 'great game' – when nineteenth-century imperial statesmen engaged one another in geopolitical chess across the 'board' of Central Asia – has been resumed in the late twentieth century with a new set of players has stuck in the minds of many media commentators, specialists and policy-makers. The great game model can be reduced to the following outline: (1) With the Soviet collapse, a vacuum has been created in the FSS. (2) This vacuum is bound to be filled with external influence. (3) Various states will take advantage of this situation to try to impose their models on the region, thereby enhancing their global power and prestige.

For policy-makers this produces an inexorable logic to promote their own state's model and to denigrate other states' models. This 'clash of models' adds a new element to the pure power politics of the original great game: now it is ideologies, not merely empires, that are the competitors. The players enlisted in the competition are Russia, Turkey and Iran, with a team of reserve players also available: the West itself (the USA and Europe), China, Saudi Arabia, Pakistan, India and others. The historicist logic of the great game, however, propels Russia, Turkey and Iran to the front line, for these are the powers that have the closest historical and cultural affinities with the region and that have in the past been most involved in Central Asian and Transcaucasian rivalries. Ideas about what these countries represent vary, of course, from analyst to analyst. In the standard Western view, Russia is the old imperial power, trying to hold on to or recover its Asian empire, but with an uncertain future ideology, Turkey is the West's proxy player, representing secularism, democracy and the market economy, while Iran stands for Islamic fundamentalism, revolution and everything anti-Western.[1] From other perspectives Turkey's role appears more sinister, as the potential leader of a new Turkic (or

---

[1] R. Cullen, 'Central Asia and the West', in M. Mandelbaum (ed.), *Central Asia and the World* (New York: Council on Foreign Relations Press, 1994), pp. 130–46. For appraisals of Russian and Turkish policies and priorities in Central Asia, see I.D. Zviagelskaia, *The Russian Policy Debate on Central Asia* (London: RIIA, Former Soviet South Paper, forthcoming 1995); and G. Winrow, *Turkey in Post-Soviet Central Asia* (London: RIIA, Former Soviet South Paper, 1995).

pan-Turkic) alliance stretching from the Bosporus to China, while Iran's view of what it has to offer is very different from the West's.

This essentially geopolitical model for the international relations of the FSS is open to criticism on many counts: for instance, it treats the new states as passive sponges absorbing foreign influence, not as active participants; it ignores the importance of economic relations and capacity in modern international relations; it grossly oversimplifies the 'characters' of the players and the nature of their interrelationship, which involves elements of cooperation as well as competition; and its fundamental assumption of a vacuum is invalid – the Soviet legacy and infrastructure continue to be a determining factor throughout the FSS.[2]

The weaknesses of the model notwithstanding, it has undoubtedly played a part in shaping the course of the opening up of the international relations of the FSS. There was a period, from late 1991 to mid-1992, when it did appear that Russia was turning its back on the region to pursue a new Euro-Atlanticist foreign policy, leaving a power vacuum to be filled.[3] Against this background there was something like a scramble for influence between Turkey and Iran, with a number of initiatives by both countries in an atmosphere of intense rivalry, heightened by the strong US support for Turkey and opposition to Iran, which was most audibly voiced by Secretary of State James Baker during his visit to the region in early 1992. There are, moreover, a few areas where the competition for influence really is a zero-sum game – the battle of the alphabets, for example, has been won by Turkey for the Latin alphabet, which proved more attractive (except in Tajikistan) than the Arabic script promoted by Iran and the Arab world (though in fact inertia and lack of resources will enable Russia's Cyrillic at least to fight a lengthy rearguard action) – but in most areas exaggerated rivalry and confrontation have already been shown to be counterproductive (the issue of the exploitation of energy resources and the routeing of pipelines is a prime example). Both Iran and Turkey realized relatively early that excessive rivalry would be detrimental to their own interests – damaging to their bilateral relations and destabilizing for the new states – and so a pattern of managed competition has emerged, with both states continuing to promote their own interests and models, but not so single-mindedly as to jeopardize relations with each other.[4]

---

[2] See Paul Goble's critique: 'The 50 Million Muslim Misunderstanding: the West and Central Asia Today', in A. Ehteshami (ed.), *From the Gulf to Central Asia: Players in the new Great Game* (Exeter: University of Exeter Press, 1994), pp. 1–5.

[3] M. Mesbahi, 'Russia and the Geopolitics of the Muslim South', in M. Mesbahi (ed.), *Central Asia and the Caucasus after the Soviet Union: Domestic and International Dynamics* (Gainesville, FL: University Press of Florida, 1994), pp. 268–319.

[4] Calabrese, op. cit., pp. 105–7; P. Robins, 'The Middle East and Central Asia', in P. Ferdinand (ed.), *The New Central Asia and its Neighbours* (London: RIIA/Pinter, 1994), pp. 70–71.

In any case, it soon became apparent that Russia's absence from the scene was only partial and temporary and that the leaders of the new states were unwilling to make a simple choice from the models on offer, thereby putting themselves in an unequal relationship with a new 'big brother'; they preferred instead to diversify their foreign relations and pursue policies according to what they perceived to be the best interests of their countries and their own authority. Broadly speaking, they have been grateful recipients of aid and investment, have welcomed the development of foreign economic relations, have opted for Russia as their main partner in security matters, have rejected outright the possibility of Islamic politics, and have shown scant enthusiasm for the development of democracy. These choices are hardly remarkable in the light of the economic and security problems confronting them, the ex-Soviet composition of most of the leaderships and the nature of state–society relations in the FSS.

Iran's position *vis-à-vis* the new great game has been ambivalent. There is no doubt that it did get drawn into the competition with Turkey – President Akbar Hashemi-Rafsanjani claimed in early 1992 that Iran offered an 'ideal model' – yet on the whole in Iran the understanding of the process of developing relations with the FSS differs from the great game scenario. Commentators and officials view Iran's new contacts with the FSS not as those of an outside power intruding into the region, but rather as a resumption of the 'natural' social, economic and cultural contacts between closely related neighbours that were artificially ruptured during the period of Russian–Soviet rule. They would see an analogy with the lifting of the iron curtain in central Europe as more pertinent than that of the great game. As a consequence Iran has often appeared a rather reluctant player in the great game and uncertain of its role in the 'clash of models' framework. While it rejects the West's stereotyped characterization of its model, its failure to produce a clear alternative is indicative of the fact that it does not perceive its role in the region in these terms (see Chapter 5).

If on the broadest level the Iranian leadership considers proximity and affinity to be a sufficient justification for its involvement in Central Asia, there are a number of specific interests and concerns that give urgency to that involvement and shape policy, and this chapter focuses on an analysis of Iran's political and security interests.

Involvement and cooperation

As was noted above, establishing cooperative regional relations is a general objective of Iranian foreign policy. Success in forging close bilateral and regional links with the FSS states would serve Iran's interests by reducing its international isolation, helping to prevent hostile encirclement and allowing it to emerge as a major regional power, since all of the FSS states are considerably smaller and weaker than itself. Attempts to establish a closer regional relationship with the Gulf Cooperation Council (GCC) states have so far been rebuffed, but Iranian leaders saw fewer obstacles towards friendly relations with the FSS states, which had had little contact with Iran in the early years of the revolution and had not been through the Gulf war. Iran had not posed a direct threat to any of them for nearly two hundred years. Tehran hoped, therefore, to be able to build up bilateral relations rapidly and join the FSS states in some form of multilateral cooperation for their mutual benefit and the furtherance of Iran's particular objectives. Iranian policy-makers had, however, underestimated the degree of suspicion felt by the FSS leaders and peoples towards their powerful Islamic revolutionary neighbour. This has gradually been diminished by sustained Iranian diplomacy, which does seem to have been effective, at least to the extent of allowing the development of normal bilateral relations with all the FSS states. Competition with Turkey for the new states' political affiliations gave an additional spur to Iranian involvement in the region.

Another motive was to improve the balance of Iran's international relations. If the overtures to the GCC and the forging of a new relationship with Russia were in part intended to counterbalance the continuing poor relations with the USA, Iran's developing relations with the FSS states can balance its relations with the Arab world and Russia. Iranian positions on the 1994 Azerbaijani oil contract and the Caspian Sea issue show how relations with the FSS states and with Russia are in balance. Similarly, relations with individual FSS states may balance those with others – Armenia and Azerbaijan are a case in point. Finally, multilateral groupings such as ECO and the Caspian Sea littoral states also have a balancing function *vis-à-vis* other multilateral regional organizations, such as GCC, the CIS, the Black Sea Cooperation Organization and the various insubstantial Eurasian and Central Asian groupings.

Regional instability

Though much larger and militarily more powerful than any of the FSS countries, Iran considers that it faces serious threats to its national security from the region.[5] With its long northern border with Armenia, Azerbaijan and Turkmenistan, its Caspian coastline, its Azerbaijani and Turkmen minorities and its geographical proximity to the Karabagh war (Georgia, Chechenia and Tajikistan are also uncomfortably close), Iran's

[5] On Iran's perceptions of the threat from the FSS, see S. Chubin, *Iran's National Security Policy: Capabilities, Intentions and Impact* (Washington DC: The Carnegie Endowment for International Peace, 1994); S.K. Sajjadpour, 'Iran, the Caucasus and Central Asia', in A. Banuazizi and M. Weiner (eds), *The New Geopolitics of Central Asia and its Borderlands* (London and New York: I.B. Tauris, 1994), p. 198; idem., '*Rabeteh-ye amniyat va tause'eh dar Asiya-ye Markazi va Qafqaz* (The Relationship between Security and Development in Central Asia and the Caucasus)', *MMAMQ*, vol. 2, no. 4 (1994), pp. 109–20. On the dynamics of conflict in the region, see V.V. Naumkin (ed.), *Central Asia and Transcaucasia: Ethnicity and Conflict* (Westport, CO: Greenwood Press, 1994).

security is, perhaps, more closely linked to the FSS states than that of any other outside country except Russia. During the Soviet period Iran faced a constant military and ideological threat from the superpower to the north. It had to accept *de facto* Soviet control of the Caspian Sea and Soviet terms for the management of the borders; it could never hope to match the USSR militarily and had to cope with intermittent Soviet support for opposition movements in Iran, particularly the communist Tudeh party. Nevertheless, the threat had become a 'known' quantity; the Soviet Union was, or appeared to be, stable. There were no Soviet internal conflicts, and in any case the tight control of the borders minimized the danger of a spillover into Iran from developments within the USSR. Generally speaking, Soviet policy towards Iran was driven more by global concerns that necessitated caution than by ideology; the Soviet threat was, if not invented, at least deliberately exploited by the Pahlavis to justify defence spending. Finally, a *modus vivendi* had been established, so that while relations sometimes deteriorated, the danger of a downward spiral into open conflict was remote. By comparison, the risks of the post-Soviet era seem at times almost to inspire in Tehran the feeling 'better the devil you know'.

The potential security threats emanating from the FSS are both direct and indirect. In the first place there are the immediate consequences of the disintegration of the Soviet security system, which left an extremely fluid and volatile situation. Iran has understandable worries about the uncertain process of the formation of national armies and security doctrines in the FSS states, the weakening or possible breakdown of border security, the dissemination of the Soviet arsenal (to local militias and gangs, as well as to new state armies), and the involvement of outside powers in new security agreements, military training and arms supply. The need for a new security system for the Caspian Sea (see below) is a related concern.

The several ongoing armed conflicts in the FSS are also a major concern for Iran. The war in Afghanistan and the 1991 Gulf war have made Iran acutely aware of the dangers and costs (e.g. refugees) arising from conflicts in neighbouring countries. In summer 1993 fighting in the Karabagh war actually reached Iran's borders, eliciting a large-scale mobilization of Iran's forces and threatening a flood of Azerbaijani refugees, driven from their homes by the victorious Armenian troops. The Karabagh war and the wars in Tajikistan, Georgia and Chechenia also pose difficulties for the Iranian government in terms of domestic public response calling for support of one or other side (the co-ethnic, co-religionist Azerbaijanis, the Islamic opposition in Tajikistan, the oppressed Muslims of Chechenia and Abkhazia), as well as in their potential for drawing in outside powers, as backers of one or other side, as actual participants, or as peace-keepers.

Less acute conflicts and disputes are also felt as dangers. Ethnic and religious tensions and unrest within the new states can elicit domestic demands for an Iranian response. Nationalism, minority demands for autonomy and independence, and irredentism may have a direct impact (as in the Azerbaijani case), but also, by example, pose a more general threat to Iran's multi-ethnic state. Calls for the revision of internal FSU boundaries are also disturbing to Iran, which would not welcome the opening of discussion about its own borders: like those of much of the Middle East, these are in some cases artificial creations cutting across ethnic, cultural, geographic and economic lines. The Iranian government regularly reaffirms its adherence to the principles of respect for internationally recognized borders, territorial integrity and non-interference in the internal affairs of other states.[6] Related to the question of border security is that of the development of organized crime and the drugs trade. The possibility of outside intervention in support of a minority (most likely in relation to the Russian minority in Central Asia) is an additional source of anxiety.

Even unrest and protest over declining socio-economic conditions or challenges to neighbouring governments' legitimacy and authority are generally unwelcome to Tehran, which is facing similar protests and challenges at home. In this sense the Iranian government's sense of its own unpopularity at home encourages it in what might appear an uncharacteristic solidarity with the predominantly conservative ex-Soviet governments of the FSS.[7] As is the case for Russia and the West, for Iran the first priority in the FSS is stability, which it sees as the precondition for the development of relations in all areas, as well as important for its own national security.

The dangers posed by regional conflicts and unrest were already becoming apparent to Iran from the late 1980s. There were riots and pogroms in all five Central Asian Republics in 1989–90,[8] but it was the outbreak of the Karabagh conflict and the burgeoning of the Azerbaijani nationalist movement, with its direct appeals to Iran's Azerbaijanis and, in January 1990, publicized violation of the Irano–Soviet border, that gave Tehran its bitterest taste of things to come and conditioned the very cautious response to the independence of the southern Soviet nations. As late as December 1991, the month of the disintegration of the USSR, an Iranian deputy foreign minister

---

[6] Ali Akbar Velayati's speech to the 49th session of the UN General Assembly (*Kayhan International*, 29 September 1994). According to S. Shahabi and F. Farhi, in 'Security Considerations and Iranian Foreign Policy', *Iranian Journal of International Affairs*, vol. 7, no. 1 (1995), p. 91, 'Iran can easily be considered a territorially satisfied state with its diplomatic and military efforts directed at guarding well-established borders and maintaining its status in a region in which territorial disputes constitute a norm'. There are, of course, Iranian irredenta in Central Asia, Transcaucasia, Iraq, the Persian Gulf, Afghanistan and even Turkey, but claims on them are made only by extreme nationalists and have no place in government policy, which gives a high priority to maintaining territorial integrity, not only in relation to its own borders, but also to those of Iraq and Afghanistan. On Iran's borders see K.L. MacLachlan (ed.), *The Boundaries of Modern Iran* (London: UCL Press, 1994).

[7] Robins, op. cit., pp. 57–61.

[8] J.S. Schoeberlein-Engel, 'Conflict in Tajikistan and Central Asia', *Harvard Middle Eastern and Islamic Review*, vol. 1, no. 2 (1994), p. 20.

was still affirming that: 'It is a fundamental policy of ours that we develop our political, economic and cultural relations with the republics within the framework of our relations with Moscow'.[9] If authoritarian ex-communist presidents and Russian-dominated CIS structures seem to provide the best guarantees of regional stability, Iran is unlikely to oppose them.

Hostile penetration

Another reason for Iran's interest in the FSS springs from its wider perception of its place in the world order. In ideological terms, the Islamic Republic still sees itself as a standard-bearer of resistance to America's neo-imperialist ambition of global domination, and as such a focus for US hostility and conspiracy. In this struggle, it alleges, the USA employs every available means: direct military pressure, mobilization of allies and proxies, and economic infiltration by Western multinational companies. Following this line of thought, the policies formulated in Washington under the rubric of containment appear as aggressive encirclement, and the opening up of the FSU to the outside world seems also to open the way for the completion of that encirclement.[10] This ideological perspective is not the only one current in Iran, but it continues to have its place in the minds of the political elite and to find expression in the media, where the entry of Western multinationals into the FSS and Turkey's regional ambitions are often reported with undisguised suspicion. Turkey is resented as the West's self-confessed proxy in the region, but Iran also has other anxieties about Turkey's role. Some of these are historical, dating back to the Ottoman-Safavi rivalry of the sixteenth and seventeenth century and to the pan-Turkism of the turn of the twentieth century. The idea of sweeping Turkish success, the spread of political neo-pan-Turkism and the establishment of a Turkic confederacy may be a phantasm, but it is one which Iran shares with both Russia and Armenia. There is a high degree of harmony between Russian, Armenian and Iranian historical stereotypes of the Turko-Mongol hordes' onslaught against Christian Russian and Armenian and Islamic Persian Indo-European civilization. Anxieties on this count helped propel Iran into the competition for influence in the FSS, which it, like Turkey, views as part of its inalienable historic and cultural hinterland. Another stems from the exclusivist nationalism of the Turkish state, which Iran views as akin to, if not directly inspiring, the destabilizing extremist nationalism prevalent in the region. Iran and Turkey's mutual suspicions and rivalry

[9] Ali Mohammad Besharati, cited in A. Ehteshami, 'New Frontiers: Iran, the GCC and the CCARS', in A. Ehteshami (ed.), op. cit., p. 98. See also *The Independent*, 3 September 1991, and *The Christian Science Monitor*, 27 September–3 October 1991.
[10] J. Calabrese, *Revolutionary Horizons: Regional Foreign Policy in Post-Khomeini Iran* (Basingstoke: Macmillan, 1994), pp. 76–8.

have, however, tended to diminish over time as each side came to perceive the limits of the other's capacity to control or even influence the region, and recognized the scope for mutually advantageous cooperation, and the need to contain their competition in order to maintain the balance of their bilateral relations.[11] Iran's fear of the flag following the trade of the multinationals has, however, been heightened by developments in the Caspian Sea (see Chapter 4). The defensive need to maintain Iran's presence and status in the region in order to frustrate America continues to be a motivating factor for active involvement.[12]

Regional priorities

Iran's conviction that the restoration of its relations with Central Asia and the Caucasus is a 'natural' restoration of its rightful place in the region combines with the specific concerns about regional balance, stability and encirclement, and its economic and cultural interests (Chapters 4 and 5) to motivate close involvement in the FSS. These factors and interests do not, however, apply uniformly to the whole region. Their nature and interaction creates an undeclared pecking order among the states based on the potential threats to Iranian security, the opportunities for economic interaction, and religious, cultural and linguistic affinity. Relations with bordering states – Armenia, Azerbaijan and Turkmenistan – are given a high priority, while the importance of Kazakhstan is enhanced by its being a Caspian littoral state. Tajikistan is relatively remote and of limited economic potential, but it is the one FSS state whose official language is closely related to Persian, and this gives it a special place in Iran's priorities. The religious bond of Islam to some extent influences Iran's relations with the six FSS states that have majority Muslim populations. The links with mainly Shi'i Azerbaijan are closest in this respect, but even though Iranian Islam may have little in common with the Islam of Kazakhstan and Kyrgyzstan, Iran still sees them as Islamic states and accordingly gives added priority to relations with them. The potential for economic cooperation, particularly in the energy sector, is an important incentive to intensify relations with Azerbaijan, Turkmenistan and Kazakhstan. Uzbekistan has no common border with Iran and has fewer energy resources, but it is the most populous of the FSS states, which makes it a large potential market for Iranian exports, and it has close historical and cultural associations with Iran. Relations with Christian Georgia, which neither shares a border with Iran nor offers immediate prospects for economic relations, are a lower priority, but its internal conflicts and their connection with instability in the North Caucasus, as well as its place on potential transit routes

---

[11] Robins, op. cit., pp. 70–1; Calabrese, op. cit., p. 107; Winrow, op. cit., p. 47.
[12] FBIS-NES-92-091, 11 May 1992.

18

linking Iran to the Black Sea, Ukraine and Russia, ensure that it is not neglected. A speculative grouping of the states according to the priority attached to them in Iranian foreign policy would be:

- Group 1: Azerbaijan, Turkmenistan
- Group 2: Armenia, Tajikistan
- Group 3: Kazakhstan, Uzbekistan
- Group 4: Kyrgyzstan, Georgia

It should also be stressed that Russia retains a higher priority than any of the FSS states, and that Iran has, in addition, forged economic links with Ukraine, which, if they develop, could produce significant results.

In the broader context of Iran's overall foreign policy, the priority given to relations with the FSS is already quite high and rising. Whereas for the West and even for Turkey (at least as far as Central Asia is concerned) the region is interesting but hardly vital, for Iran (as for Russia) its close proximity and potentially infectious instability, as well as the opportunities it offers, make it genuinely important.

3 BILATERAL POLITICAL RELATIONS

This chapter focuses on the pattern of Iran's diplomatic relations with the FSS states and the agreements signed. Many of these agreements concern economic and cultural relations, but since many remain unfulfilled, their diplomatic significance is at this stage as great as that of their substance. It is noteworthy, if not surprising, that there have been almost no agreements in the security field (by contrast, Turkey is assisting several FSS states with military training and specialists).[1] In the first place it is unlikely that any of the FSS states would agree to significant security links with Iran, were they to be proposed; and in any case, as was suggested above, Iran seems to hold the view (if not to publicize it) that the FSS states' bilateral agreements with Russia and CIS security structures best serve its regional security interests of stability, maintenance of borders and exclusion of hostile powers. Second, in so far as Iran sees a security role for itself in the region, it appears to do so in terms of (1) mediation of regional conflicts, which could extend to a possible peacekeeping role, and (2) multilateral organizations. The potential extension of the functions of ECO to include a security dimension would seem to be a logical outcome of Iran's expressed hopes for a future linkage between ECO and the GCC, though it has not been proposed so far.[2] Iran has also put security on the agenda for cooperation by the five Caspian littoral states. In view of this, and of the importance attached to regional cooperation and multilateral organizations in all areas of foreign relations, ECO and Caspian Sea cooperation could have been included in this chapter, but as their primary functions remain economic, they are discussed in Chapter 4.

The first developments in bilateral relations with the FSS countries predate Iranian recognition of their independence, which came only in late December 1991. In November, however, agreements were reached on opening new border crossings with Turkmenistan and Azerbaijan, and in the same month Foreign Minister Ali Akbar

---

[1] The solitary exception being a letter of understanding for political, military and border cooperation with Turkmenistan (FBIS-NES-94-005, 7 January 1994).
[2] K.L. Afrasiabi, *After Khomeini: New Directions in Iran's Foreign Policy* (Boulder, CO: Westview Press, 1994), p. 123.

Velayati made a ten-day visit to the Soviet Union, including Central Asia, and reached agreement (with Russian approval) on opening Iranian consulates in all six 'Muslim' republics and on the expansion of cultural, economic, political and technical cooperation. Agreement on opening embassies was reached with Azerbaijan, Tajikistan, Turkmenistan, Kazakhstan and Armenia by early 1992, with Uzbekistan and Kyrgyzstan in May, and with Georgia in June of the same year.

A series of high-level bilateral visits and meetings was also initiated, while meetings of ECO, OIC and other bodies (see Chapter 4) gave additional opportunities for discussions between ministers and presidents. A chronology of these visits and meetings for the period 1992–4 conveys a sense of the intensity and character of the developing relations.[3]

January 1992 The Iranian foreign minister Ali Akbar Velayati and the Turkmen president Saparmurad Niyazov officially opened a new border crossing.

February 1992 The Armenian foreign minister Raffi Hovannisian met with the Iranian president and foreign minister to discuss the Karabagh conflict and to reach agreement on border relations, joint investments, Armenian purchases of Iranian natural gas, and the establishment of a refinery. The transport ministers of Iran and Kazakhstan agreed on cooperation and the establishment of a joint permanent transportation committee.

March 1992 Iran and Azerbaijan agreed to expand telecommunications links. Iran and Turkmenistan signed a trade agreement said to be worth $80 million for the exchange of Turkmen goods and raw materials for Iranian foodstuffs. The leader of Tajikistan's Democratic Party visited Tehran and called for the expansion of ties.

April 1992 Kazakhstan's minister of culture and Turkmenistan's education minister visited Tehran, the latter visit resulting in the signature of a letter of understanding on cooperation. The Iranian oil minister and a deputy foreign minister visited Ashgabat and reached agreement on easing visa requirements and opening two new border checkpoints to facilitate trade and travel. Tajikistan's minister of economic affairs visited Tehran to discuss joint investment in the agricultural, industrial and energy sectors.

May 1992 In Ashgabat for a conference on economic cooperation between Central Asian states, Akbar Hashemi-Rafsanjani signed a treaty of friendship with Turkmenistan and reached agreement on the construction of a gas pipeline through Iran to Turkey. Earlier in the month agreements had been signed for a joint Iran–Turkmenistan economic commission, for trade (including $34 million in Iranian food exports) and for a $50 million Iranian credit to Turkmenistan. Iran and Azerbaijan signed agreements on judicial and legal matters, on expanding cooperation in the oil and gas sectors (including setting up

---

[3] The chronology was compiled by Gudrun Persson on the basis of the FBIS *Daily Reports* for Central Eurasia and for the Near East and South Asia.

a joint exploration company, the annual export of one billion cubic metres of Iranian gas to Azerbaijan and Nakhichevan), on opening radio and television offices in each other's countries and on maintaining friendly and neighbourly relations. Similar agreements on friendly relations, the expansion of ties and cooperation were also signed with Armenia, leading to the opening of a pontoon bridge on the River Aras to link the two countries. Iran's and Tajikistan's ministers of culture agreed to expand ties. A tripartite agreement on radio and television cooperation was signed between Iran, Tajikistan and Azerbaijan.

June 1992   Tajikistan's ministers of education, the economy and finance visited Tehran. A memorandum of understanding was signed on scientific and cultural cooperation. The Georgian prime minister visited Iran for talks with the president and foreign minister. Agreements were signed on communications and transport, trade (including Iranian gas exports), political consultations and the easing of visa requirements. The Iranian health minister, Reza Malekzadeh, visited Central Asia, where he signed four memoranda of understanding. President Rakhman Nabiev of Tajikistan visited Tehran and signed a protocol on economic cooperation. Iran agreed a $50 million credit to allow Tajikistan to buy Iranian industrial facilities.

July 1992   Iran and Turkmenistan signed seventeen economic protocols (said to be worth $30 million) and three agricultural protocols. The transport ministers of Iran and Tajikistan signed a memorandum of understanding on cooperation over road, rail and air transport.

August 1992   The Azerbaijani foreign minister visited Tehran (the first such high-level visit since the Azerbaijani Popular Front came to power in March) and agreed to cooperate with Iran in Caspian oil exploration. Later in the month Heydar Aliyev, leader of the Nakhichevan Autonomous Republic of Azerbaijan, also visited Tehran and signed agreements on economic cooperation, broadcasting, and the opening of an Iranian consulate in Nakhichevan and an Azerbaijani consulate in Tabriz. A Kyrgyz parliamentary delegation visited Tehran and signed agreements on cooperation in parliamentary affairs, commerce, transport and telecommunications. President Saparmurad Niyazov visited Tehran for further talks on the gas pipeline project and cooperation in the oil industry.

September 1992   At a conference in Tehran on energy cooperation in the FSS, Azerbaijan and Iran agreed on the annual supply of 40,000 megawatts of electricity to Nakhichevan by Iran, and on the construction of a bridge at Khoda Afarin on the River Aras. Iran and Tajikistan agreed to ease visa requirements. The Tajik minister of culture visited Tehran and met the Iranian president and foreign minister.

November 1992   President Nursultan Nazarbaev of Kazakhstan visited Tehran and signed an agreement on mutual understanding and cooperation covering scientific and technical cooperation, shipping and parliamentary relations. Agreements were signed with Kyrgyzstan for oil cooperation, and with Azerbaijan for economic, scientific and cultural cooperation. Islam Karimov, president of Uzbekistan, visited Tehran and signed a joint statement on economic, cultural, and communications and transport cooperation.

December 1992 Turkmenistan's foreign minister visited Tehran for discussions with Akbar Hashemi-Rafsanjani and Ali Akbar Velayati on road and railway construction, the gas pipeline and water reservoirs.

January 1993 President Edouard Shevardnadze of Georgia visited Iran and signed agreements for friendship and cooperation in the fields of parliamentary and economic affairs, transport and communications. Ali Akbar Velayati visited Turkmenistan, Uzbekistan and Kazakhstan.

February 1993 Iranian and Kazakhstani ministers of labour signed a memorandum of understanding on technical and vocational training and work safety measures.

March 1993 The ministers of culture of Iran and Turkmenistan signed an agreement on cultural ties. Heydar Aliyev again visited Tehran from Nakhichevan for talks with the Iranian president and foreign minister.

April 1993 The vice-president of Turkmenistan held talks in Tehran with the Iranian vice-president and foreign minister on the occasion of the first session of the joint economic committee.

May 1993 Ali Akbar Velayati signed agreements in Tbilisi in the industrial, economic, agricultural, trade, cultural and telecommunications fields.

June 1993 The Iranian minister of culture, Ali Larijani, visited Azerbaijan and signed an agreement on cultural ties. Kazakhstan's minister of culture visited Tehran, as did Askar Akaev, president of Kyrgyzstan; this led to the signature of seven agreements on transport, banking and tourism. Akbar Hashemi-Rafsanjani offered Iranian assistance in the fields of oil exploration, extraction and refining. Iran and Uzbekistan signed agreements on cooperation in rail, road and air communications.

July 1993 Ali Akbar Velayati visited Azerbaijan at the invitation of the newly installed President Heydar Aliyev and signed a memorandum on mutual relations.

September 1993 The vice-president and fuel minister of Turkmenistan visited Tehran. An agreement was signed on technical cooperation.

October 1993 Akbar Hashemi-Rafsanjani and Kazakhstan's minister for energy and fuel resources held talks on transport and oil-sector cooperation on the occasion of the first session of their countries' joint committee for economic and commercial cooperation. The Iranian president made a nine-day tour of Uzbekistan, Turkmenistan, Kyrgyzstan, Kazakhstan and Azerbaijan. A further agreement on the transport of gas from Turkmenistan through Iran was signed, and the new Tajan bridge joining the two countries was inaugurated. Iran and Kazakhstan agreed to ease visa restrictions. Several agreements on transport cooperation were also signed during the tour. Later in the month Iran and Azerbaijan agreed to allow their nationals to stay for up to fifteen days in each other's country without a visa.

December 1993   The Azerbaijani foreign minister held talks with his Iranian counterpart and the president in Tehran.

January 1994   The Turkmen president, Saparmurad Niyazov, and the ministers of culture and foreign affairs visited Tehran for talks on implementing the oil and gas agreements. Agreements were signed on telecommunications (which will facilitate contact between Iran and all the Central Asian states), and on political, military and border cooperation.

May 1994   The prime minister of Kazakhstan visited Tehran and signed letters of understanding in the industrial and agricultural fields.

June 1994   President Heydar Aliyev of Azerbaijan visited Tehran for talks on economic, technical, commercial and industrial ties.

July 1994   The Iranian oil minister, Gholamreza Aqazadeh, held talks in Ashgabat on the gas agreement.

August 1994   Ali Akbar Velayati made a nine-day tour of Kazakhstan, Kyrgyzstan, Turkmenistan, Uzbekistan and Azerbaijan. Presidents Saparmurad Niyazov of Turkmenistan and Akbar Hashemi-Rafsanjani of Iran symbolically began construction of the $7 billion gas pipeline to transport Turkmen gas to Europe via Iran and Turkey (real construction was scheduled to begin in May 1995). Representatives from Russia, Turkey and Kazakhstan were also present. The construction costs for the Iranian section of the pipeline were estimated at $3.5 billion.

September 1994   Iran and Georgia agreed to expand economic ties. In 1995, 30 million cubic metres of Iranian gas will be traded for Georgian goods.

October 1994   Iran and Turkmenistan agreed to ease visa restrictions. The Iranian oil minister and subsequently the president visited Ashgabat and agreed further oil and gas cooperation, including a pipeline to transport Turkmen oil to world markets via Iran. Iran, Russia and Turkmenistan agreed to set up a consortium for oil and gas exploration and exploitation in Turkmenistan. Iran and Kazakhstan agreed to expand trade, establish a joint chamber of commerce and cooperate in metals extraction and transport.

November 1994   Iran and Azerbaijan agreed to the National Iranian Oil Company taking a five per cent share in the oil consortium (formed in September 1994).

This intense diplomatic initiative has achieved a high level of contact and agreement between Iran and the FSS states. This in itself constitutes a success for the Islamic Republic, which is now better understood and less feared by its northern neighbours, and consequently less isolated internationally than before. This success must, however, be qualified. First, it should not be forgotten that Iran was not alone in launching a diplomatic drive towards the FSS states in this period. Turkey moved faster and with greater success than Iran, especially in 1991–2. It recognized the independence of the new states earlier, secured agreements and set up embassies sooner, received a warmer welcome in most of the FSS states, and persuaded most of them to express support for the Turkish model of development and to adopt the Latin alphabet.[4] Only in Armenia and Tajikistan were Iran's overtures received more favourably than Turkey's. The other point to note is that bilateral relations have not developed with the same ease and speed in all cases. Tehran is probably quite satisfied with the pace and character of its developing relations with Kazakhstan, Georgia and Kyrgyzstan, and relations with Turkmenistan have evolved quite rapidly and without a serious hitch. Relations with Azerbaijan, however, have gone through some difficult phases, and those with Uzbekistan have developed more slowly than Iran would have liked (Tashkent was the last Central Asian capital to open an Iranian embassy) and by no means without friction. Erevan and Tehran seem generally to have found a good understanding, but the Karabagh war has from time to time put a serious strain on the developing friendship. In the case of Tajikistan the promising start was set back almost to square one by the civil war.

Impediments to the development of bilateral relations

Iran has faced a number of obstacles in developing relations with the FSS states. Some of these are more or less general. There is a universal fear and rejection of Islamic fundamentalism and political Islam among the leaderships of the FSS states; ex-Soviet *nomenklatura* and anti-communist nationalist elites share the same commitment to secular government. The Islamic Republic of Iran is viewed by most Central Asians with little enthusiasm as a model, or even as a potential partner and source of assistance, at least according to a 1993 opinion poll in Kazakhstan and Uzbekistan.[5] Even the Islamic opposition, where it has had a chance to form and express itself, does not look to Iran. Only in mainly Shi'i Azerbaijan is there a small pro-Iranian Islamic party. Ironically, the fear of Iran as a source of Islamic sedition and a representative of non-secular government is weakest in the 'Christian' countries, Georgia and Armenia, whose Islamic anxieties are focused respectively on internal minorities and on Turkey and Azerbaijan.

Quite apart from the Islamic factor, Iran is viewed with caution because of its size, strength and proximity, and because for many of the FSS states it represents a former oppressive foreign overlord (a lesson thoroughly inculcated through Soviet and nationalist historiography). None of the FSS states would welcome the emergence of Iran as a new regional hegemon; in the case of Kazakhstan and Uzbekistan, this would

---

[4] G. Winrow, *Turkey in Post-Soviet Central Asia* (London: RIIA, Former Soviet South Paper, 1995), pp. 13–14.
[5] N. Lubin, 'Islam and Ethnic Identity in Central Asia: A View from Below', in Y. Ro'i (ed.), *Muslim Eurasia: Conflicting Legacies* (London: Frank Cass, the Cummings Centre Series, 1995), pp. 61, 66–7.

clash with their own ambitions for regional status. Between Iranians and the Turkic peoples there is also an atavistic mutual ambivalence inherited from their centuries-long relationship, which has contained as many elements of tension and conflict as of harmony and creative exchange. Historically Iran had far from amicable relations with the Turkmen nomads across its northeastern border, but in the contemporary period ambivalence causes most tension with the Azerbaijanis and the Uzbeks.

Azerbaijan

Relations between Iran and Azerbaijan have been complicated by a number of issues. Ultimately these boil down to questions of identity and nationality in both countries,[6] but the tense dynamics of the relationship derive in large part from the fluidity and volatility of post-Soviet Azerbaijani politics. Iran professes itself a multi-ethnic Islamic society, but there are strict limits on the degree of autonomy allowed to its minority nationalities. With an Azerbaijani population variously reckoned at between 10 and 20 million (a substantial proportion of the entire population), mostly living in the northwest, all Tehran governments are concerned about separatist Azerbaijani nationalism. So far there is no evidence of widespread support for this in Iran; there were anti-government riots in Tabriz, as in many other Iranian cities, in 1994, but the grievances seem to have been socio-economic and cultural (frustration with Islamic social restrictions) rather than nationalist. Iranian Azerbaijanis have a distinct and more Iranian sense of identity than their northern co-ethnics, and there can be no doubt that seventy years of Soviet rule have left significant differences in outlook and aspiration between them. Azerbaijan, too, has its minorities, among them the Talesh, an Iranian people concentrated near the border with Iran, but the short-lived 1993 Talesh separatist movement attracted little popular support and received no backing from Tehran.

The historical, cultural and political debates surrounding the issue of Azerbaijani identity cannot be explored here,[7] but the central arguments can be given in broad outline. Most Iranians consider that their Azerbaijani fellow-citizens are, and for centuries have been, fully accepted as part of the population of Iran (some reckon them to be Turkophone Iranians rather than a separate nationality), and point to the thorough

---

[6] G. Fuller, *The Center of the Universe: the Geopolitics of Iran* (Boulder, CO: Westview Press, 1990), pp. 172–6.
[7] T. Swietochowski, *Russian Azerbaijan, 1905–1920: the Snaping of National Identity in a Muslim Community* (Cambridge: Cambridge University Press, 1985); S.T. Hunter, 'Azerbaijan: Search for Identity and New Partners', in I. Bremmer and R. Taras (eds), *Nations and Politics in the Soviet Successor States* (Cambridge: Cambridge University Press, 1993), pp. 225–60; A.L. Altstadt, *The Azerbaijani Turks: Power and Identity under Russian Rule* (Stanford, CA; Hoover Institution Press, 1992).

integration of Azerbaijanis into society (including in every sector of the national elite) and to the great contribution of Azerbaijanis to Iran's modern history and culture. According to this view, Iran's Caucasian provinces (among them those that were later incorporated to form northern Azerbaijan) were forcibly separated from Iran by Russian military might in the early nineteenth century and any reunification should take the form of northern Azerbaijan rejoining its historic, cultural and religious home, Iran.

The Azerbaijani nationalist interpretation is very different. It holds that Azerbaijanis are ethnic Turks (or, according to another variant, a composite 'Caspian' nationality originating in the Caucasian Albanians) and views Azerbaijan as a historic country which has suffered a series of foreign conquests and occupations. Iranian rule, like Russian rule, was imposed by force and still holds sway in southern Azerbaijan. Reunification should take the form of the 'liberation' of southern Azerbaijan to unite with the north in a single Azerbaijani nation-state. In addition, most educated Azerbaijanis are secular in outlook, identify themselves with Western culture and ideals and are deeply suspicious that Islamic Iran has hegemonic ambitions towards their country, that it actively cooperates with Moscow and Erevan against Azerbaijan, that it is training Islamic activists to spread sedition in Azerbaijan, and so on. Allegations of this kind appear regularly in the Azerbaijani media, but are uncorroborated by credible evidence and denied by Iran.[8]

At the level of interstate relations, such ideas have considerable potential for tension and confrontation. It was noted above that the upsurge of Azerbaijani nationalism and the border violations in the late Soviet period were a source of anxiety to the Iranian government. The rise of the Azerbaijani Popular Front and Azerbaijan's determinedly pro-Turkish position in the immediate post-Soviet period caused continuing concern, though Iranian–Azerbaijani relations also developed quite rapidly. It was, however, the period of Azerbaijani Popular Front government (March 1992 to June 1993) that most disturbed Tehran. The Popular Front leader, Abulfaz Elchibey, was an outspoken nationalist who had often called for greater freedom for Azerbaijanis in Iran and for their reunification with northern Azerbaijan. Initially he pursued an outspoken anti-Iranian, anti-Russian foreign policy, looking to Turkey and the West for support for an independent democratic Azerbaijan. Later in his presidency his approach towards Iran became more conciliatory,[9] but there was still a marked chill in relations until Heydar Aliyev, leader of Nakhichevan (with whom Iran had already been cultivating close relations), came to power on the back of Suret Huseinov's coup.

---

[8] FBIS-SOV-95-020-S, 31 January 1995; FBIS-SOV-95-036, 23 February 1995; *Kayhan International*, 6 November 1994.
[9] S.K. Sajjadpour, 'Iran, the Caucasus and Central Asia', in A. Banuazizi and M. Weiner (eds), *The New Geopolitics of Central Asia and its Borderlands* (London and New York: I.B. Tauris, 1994), p. 203.

In the past Aliyev had also made remarks that would alarm any Iranian government,[10] but as president he has seen Azerbaijan's best interest in maintaining balanced relations with Russia and Iran, as well as Turkey. Tehran has responded by offering him full support during the crises of September 1994 and March 1995. Even so relations have not been entirely smooth; Aliyev's ready acceptance of Washington's rejection of Iranian participation in an Azerbaijani oil consortium (see Chapter 4) has angered Tehran, which has in turn blocked the export of a range of goods and demanded that Azerbaijan start to pay for Iranian electricity supplies to Nakhichevan.

Iran's position towards Azerbaijan and its Azerbaijani minority is likely to remain ambivalent. So far the emphasis has been on positive engagement: there is more officially sanctioned use of the Azerbaijani language in Iran now than before 1989; border and visa controls are looser; Azerbaijan has been allowed to open a consulate in Tabriz; and each country has given some access to the other's broadcast media. Even so, Tehran keeps a close watch on developments and would not allow the uncontrolled expansion of contact between northern and southern Azerbaijanis.

Uzbekistan

Some of the hurdles facing Iran's relations with Uzbekistan are similar to those with Azerbaijan. Although there is no Uzbek minority in Iran, there is a minority issue at stake, that of the Tajiks (close ethnic and linguistic kin to the Iranians) of Uzbekistan, as well as a broader issue of nationality and identity.[11] Iranian nationalists tend to view Uzbekistan as an artificial modern creation, and reckon that Tajiks make up a much larger proportion of the population than the Soviet censuses suggest and that many Uzbeks are really Turkophone Tajiks. They cherish Bukhara and Samarqand as two cradles of Islamic Persian civilization and feel an emotional tie to this part of a historic and cultural greater Iran dating back to pre-Islamic times. Uzbek nationalists, on the other hand, see their country as a historic centre for a distinct Central Asian, Turanian or Turkestani civilization fusing Turkic and Persian elements. They emphasize their country's greatness at the time of Timur (Tamburlane) and argue that Tajiks are really Persianized Uzbeks. While neither side has irredentist claims on the other's territory, the wrangle over the historical and cultural heritage remains an irritant; this is given

[10] T. Swietochowski, 'The Spirit of Baku', *Central Asia Monitor*, 4 (1993), p. 19; I.D. Zviagelskaia, 'Central Asia and Transcaucasia: New Geopolitics', in V.V. Naumkin (ed.), *Central Asia and Transcaucasia: Ethnicity and Conflict* (Westport, CO: Greenwood Press, 1994), p. 144.

[11] Schoeberlein-Engel, op. cit.; V.Ya. Porkhomovsky, 'Historical Origins of Interethnic Conflicts in Central Asia and Transcaucasia', in Naumkin (ed.), op. cit., pp. 11–21; E. Naby, 'The Emerging Central Asia: Ethnic and Religious Factions', in M. Mesbahi (ed.), *Central Asia and the Caucasus after the Soviet Union: Domestic and International Dynamics* (Gainesville, FL: University Press of Florida, 1994).

contemporary relevance by Uzbek suspicions of potential Iranian support for Tajik nationalism and Iranian concern about Uzbek suppression of Tajik rights and designs on Tajikistan.

Such controversies need not have disturbed the course of state-to-state relations, if there had been more trust and tact between the leaderships, but Islam Karimov exceeds other Central Asian leaders in his antipathy towards Islamic fundamentalism and has made little secret of his suspicion of the Islamic Republic's ambitions in Central Asia. Not only has he been reluctant to develop friendly relations with Iran, but he has also criticized President Saparmurad Niyazov of Turkmenistan for drawing too close to Iran.[12] Iranian diplomacy has gradually worn down his resistance and relations have developed, but there have been errors of tact on the Iranian side too, notably in a speech in Tashkent by Ali Akbar Velayati that smacked of cultural hegemonism and elicited an angry response in the Uzbek media. In 1994 the Iranian media urged the government to cancel an official visit because of Uzbekistan's close links with Israel and interference in Tajikistan.[13] If relations are more or less normal and growing, they are scarcely cordial. Islam Karimov delivered Iran another slap in the face when Uzbekistan became the only country apart from Israel to voice some support (subsequently retracted) for the US sanctions against Iran announced in May 1995.[14]

Mediating regional conflicts

Iran's anxieties about regional instability are exacerbated by the fact that there is very little it can do to control or reduce it. Regular exhortations about the perils of extremist exclusive nationalism and the virtues of tolerant inclusive Islam apparently fall on deaf ears, while acquiescence in the rule of authoritarian governments and the effective Russian military monopoly is more a passive acceptance of an inevitable and lesser evil than an active policy. With regard to the two armed conflicts in the FSS that affect Iran's interests most closely, Tehran has attempted a more positive contribution to finding a settlement.[15]

---

[12] *Nezavisimaya Gazeta*, 21 June 1994, cited in *Current Digest of the Post-Soviet Press*, vol. 46, no. 25 (1994), p. 22.

[13] *Le Monde*, 11 August 1994.

[14] Ibid., 8 May 1995.

[15] M. Mohsenin and H.S. Abedin, '*Bohran-ha-ye mantaqeh-'i va talash-ha-ye sazandeh-ye Jomhuri-ye Eslami-ye Iran* (Regional Crises and the Constructive Endeavours of the Islamic Republic of Iran)', *MMAMQ*, vol. 3, no. 6 (1994), pp. 1–8.

The Mountainous Karabagh Conflict

The Karabagh war represents the clearest and most direct threat to Iran's national security to emerge across its northern borders since the 1940s. The fighting actually reached the Iranian–Azerbaijani border in summer 1993, threatening to send a mass of Azerbaijani refugees into Iran and eliciting a major Iranian military mobilization, as well as a costly large-scale refugee relief programme. The war has accelerated the scarcely controlled militarization of the region, drawing in foreign mercenaries (including Afghan Mojahedin), and threatening to precipitate a military confrontation between Russia and Turkey. It has greatly complicated relations with Armenia and Azerbaijan, with both of which Iran seeks friendly expanded links, and has domestic repercussions among Iranian Azerbaijanis and Armenians.

For all the above reasons, Iran has a keen interest in seeing a settlement of the conflict and has expended considerable diplomatic efforts towards this end.[16] Tehran's only significant advantage as a mediator has been the perception in both Erevan and Baku (at least prior to Abulfaz Elchibey's election as president) that it has followed a more consistent and less partisan policy than either Ankara (which openly takes the Azerbaijani side) or Moscow (which has shifted tack several times since the outbreak of the conflict in 1988 and is believed by both parties to be manipulating the conflict for its own advantage). Azerbaijani nationalists, however, accuse Iran of bias towards Armenia, and the Popular Front government pushed hard to have the CSCE take on the mediating role. Erevan has generally welcomed Tehran's efforts, but Armenian battlefield successes following hard on the heels of Iranian-brokered cease-fires, the 1993 Armenian offensive that reached Iran's borders and the shooting down of an Iranian aircraft over Karabagh in March 1994 have all strained relations. Overall, Iran's attempts at mediation met with as little success as those of most other would-be mediators (Turkey, CSCE, Kazakhstan, CIS), but any disappointment at not being the successful peace-maker is probably outweighed by relief that the May 1994 Russian-brokered cease-fire is still holding. Iran has stressed that it will welcome any peaceful solution of the conflict, regardless of the mediator.

The principal Iranian initiatives can be grouped into three periods. As early as November 1991, in a conversation with the Armenian foreign minister, Ali Akbar Velayati offered Iran's assistance in helping resolve the conflict. This offer was not, however, taken up at the time.

The second and most concentrated period of Iranian mediation took place between February and May 1992. These efforts led to two cease-fires (both of very short dura-

---

[16] E. Fuller, 'Russia, Turkey, Iran, and the Karabagh Mediation Process', *RFE/RL Research Report*, vol. 3, no. 8 (1994), pp. 31–6; S.K. Sajjadpour, op. cit., pp. 206–7.

tion) and a tripartite presidential summit in Tehran, but the initiative broke down with the Armenian capture of Shusha and Lachin.

The third phase of Iranian mediation took place in early 1994. The initiative was coordinated with Russian efforts, but the Iranian participation had faded out before the cease-fire of May 1994.

Tajikistan

The close ethnic and linguistic kinship of Iranians and Tajiks lends Tajikistan a special interest for the Iranian government and public. Relations, particularly in the literary-cultural sphere, developed rapidly until the 1992 outbreak of the political conflict that rapidly escalated into civil war.[17] The sense of affinity with the Tajiks, as well as the close connection between Tajik and Afghan instability, has made the conflict in this remote country feel quite immediate to Iranians. Moreover, because a part of the Tajik opposition is Islamist, and because the conflict was widely presented (especially in Russian and Uzbekistan) as a battle between secularism and Islamic fundamentalism, there was considerable international interest in Iran's position. The line adopted by Tehran has been cautious – avoiding bias towards either side – and shows that stability has been put before ideology in relations with FSS states.[18]

The Iranian government at first reacted sharply to Russian backing for the ex-communist Khojand-Kulab faction, but subsequently shied away from potential confrontation and cooperated with the UN, Russia and other countries in the negotiations leading to the September 1994 cease-fire, signed in Tehran. Iran played an important role in these negotiations, which have earned it international plaudits as a mediator. Iran also offered to contribute troops to a UN peace-keeping force. Probably the experience gained in the unsuccessful 1992 Karabagh mediation, which was criticized in some quarters as naive and over-ambitious, was invaluable in the Tajik case.[19]

Neither the Karabagh nor the Tajik conflict is resolved, but the process of escalation has been reversed in both cases, and the prospect of the conflicts spreading out, or drawing outside states into confrontation, has faded. The small steps towards peace taken in 1994 are sufficient to make Iran feel much less threatened by these conflicts than in the summer of 1993.

[17] O. Roy, *The Civil War in Tajikistan: Causes and Implications* (Washington DC: United States Institute of Peace, 1993); N. Jawad and S. Tadjbakhsh, *Tajikistan: a Forgotten Civil War* (London: Minority Rights Group, International Report 94/6, 1995).
[18] Roy, op. cit., pp. 24–5.
[19] Jawad and Tadjbakhsh, op. cit., pp. 17–18.

4 ECONOMIC RELATIONS

Iran's economic interests and objectives in its relations with the FSS are in line with those of its general foreign economic policy (see Chapter 1).[1] There is a strong emphasis on the benefits of cooperation and mutual self-reliance. Close linkages are made between economic and political stability and security, between economic development and social and cultural development, and between economic and political relations and the development of regional trust and stability. The search for markets for Iran's exports, both energy and non-oil, is an additional objective, though less heavily emphasized in policy statements. In the context of the FSS, efforts to achieve these goals have focused on a number of areas:

(1) The oil and gas sectors seem to offer the potential for mutually advantageous cooperation.
(2) ECO is viewed as a major vehicle for mobilizing and organizing cooperation in the economic and other fields, with an eventual Islamic common market as a long-term goal.
(3) Iran also has high hopes of the nascent cooperation between the Caspian Sea littoral states.
(4) Last, but by no means least, Iran considers the opening of the FSS to present it with a very significant long-term potential to restore its historic geo-economic function as a north-south, east-west transit route linking Europe, the Middle East, the CIS countries, East and South Asia.

[1] For statements of policy see Akbar Hashemi-Rafsanjani's message to the January 1994 seminar on 'Appraisal of Development Trends in Central Asia and the Caucasus', in S.R. Mousavi, *'Negahi beh seminar-e beinolmellali "Bar-rasi-ye ravand-e tause'eh dar Asiya-ye Markazi va Qafqaz"* (A Look at the International Seminar 'Research on the Development Process in Central Asia and the Caucasus)', *MMAMQ*, vol. 2, no. 4 (1994), pp. 2–4; Ali Akbar Velayati's speech to the 49th session of the UN General Assembly, *Kayhan International*, 29 September 1994; Deputy Foreign Minister Abbas Maleki, *'Seh zamineh-ye asasi-ye maured-e tavajjoh-e Jomhuri-ye Islami-ye Iran jehat-e tause'eh va hamkari dar Asiya-ye Markazi* (The Islamic Republic of Iran's Three Fundamental and Noteworthy Grounds with Respect to Development and Cooperation in Central Asia)', *MMAMQ*, vol. 2, no. 2 (1993), pp. 230–3. See also P. Feuilherade in *The Guardian*, 14 February 1992; J. Calabrese, *Revolutionary Horizons: Regional Foreign Policy in Post-Khomeini Iran* (Basingstoke: Macmillan, 1994), pp. 79–81.

There are, however, a number of obstacles in the way of the development of economic relations with the region. Some of these have to do with the general problems of developing relations with the post-Soviet economies, others are specific to Iran and the FSS, notably the general orientation of the FSS economies towards the FSU and the inadequacies of the infrastructural links with Iran. The most fundamental impediment, however, is the limited compatibility of the Iranian and FSS economies. Despite the considerable diversity among the FSS economies, it is broadly true of all of them, and to a lesser extent of Iran, that their basic economic task is to restructure centralized largely state-owned economies towards private ownership and market economics. To achieve this all need large-scale outside investment. Iran is hardly better able to provide this investment for the FSS states than they are to help Iran with its own investment needs. No amount of cooperation and mutual self-reliance can disguise this unpalatable truth. The FSS states are, therefore increasingly striving to establish direct relations with the Western and East Asian countries that have the capacity to invest.[2] Iran's own private investment potential is by no means insignificant, but hitherto the government has been unable to create the necessary financial and economic environment to encourage domestic savings. In the longer term, however, if the economy stabilizes and external factors (such as world oil prices and US policy) become more favourable, Iran could make a significant contribution to investment in the FSS.

Trade

The development of trade relations has been an important subject in negotiations and agreements (see Chapter 3) between Iran and the FSS states. These have already significantly widened the opportunities for commercial exchange. The creation of new border crossings, the opening of embassies and consulates, the easing and in some cases removal of visa restrictions for drivers, visitors and traders, the creation of joint economic committees and chambers of commerce, the establishment of a Central Asian Trade Bank and the opening of branches of Iranian banks in FSS states all assist in the growth of commercial relations. In this respect the Iranian and FSS governments have made a serious effort to create some of the necessary conditions for growing trade. Progress has not been even – matters are probably furthest advanced with Azerbaijan, Armenia, Turkmenistan and Kazakhstan – and there have been hitches; for a time Iranian and Azerbaijani border guards were observing different weekends and Azerbaijan's Astara authorities were levying a local tax on Iranian motor vehicles.[3] The necessary commercial infrastructure to support Iranian businesses in the FSS is

[2] S. Islam, 'Capitalism on the Silk Route?', in M. Mandelbaum (ed.), *Central Asia and the World* (New York: Council on Foreign Relations Press, 1994), pp. 147–76.
[3] FBIS-SOV-95-059, 28 March 1995.

still only partly in place and there have been numerous complaints about inflated road transport costs,[4] but the momentum is continuing and mechanisms for raising and resolving problems are gradually coming into existence and beginning to function.

Iran has also expended considerable effort on organizing trade fairs and exhibitions in FSS countries. These provide the opportunity for Iranian firms to advertise their goods and services, and also to shop for Central Asian goods and products. Iran's main exports are foodstuffs, vehicles, light industrial goods, building materials, consumer goods and textiles, garments and footwear. There is some demand in Iran's diversifying manufacturing sector for FSS raw materials (cotton, asbestos, steel), and there is a market in Iran for some other FSS exports (industrial plant, vehicles, wheat, beef, ironware). There is also trade in oil and gas – Iran exports gas to Georgia and Azerbaijan (and is building a pipeline to Armenia) and imports diesel fuel from Azerbaijan; with Turkmenistan it swaps oil for gas.[5]

There is, therefore, the potential for considerable expansion in trade between Iran and the FSS countries, though whether they constitute the potential $8–10 billion market for Iranian exports claimed by the minister of economy and finance, Mohsen Nurbakhsh, remains to be seen.[6] Current levels of trade are quite modest: in 1992–3 Iran's exports to the whole CIS amounted to $218 million (60 per cent of which went to Russia) and its imports to $518 million (1.8 per cent of Iran's total imports). Apart from Russia, the main trade partners are the neighbouring FSS states: Azerbaijan, Armenia and Turkmenistan.[7]

Iran's commercial relations with the Transcaucasus have been significantly distorted by political factors. Azerbaijan's Autonomous Republic of Nakhichevan has been heavily dependent on Iranian imports because of the blockade imposed by Armenia. Iran has also provided energy, aid and a land link with Azerbaijan proper. The blockade of Nakhichevan was itself a response to Azerbaijan's blockade of Armenia, imposed in late 1989, which cut off Armenia's main links with the FSU (the alternatives through Georgia had less capacity and were also interrupted by Georgia's troubles). Trade between Iran and Armenia has increased fifteen-fold in the past four years because of this blockade, allowing Iran to become Armenia's second trading partner (after Russia) – a considerable achievement, bearing in mind the fact that there was not even a direct link between them in the Soviet period. Iran is currently building a pipeline and electricity line to enable it to supply a part of Armenia's desperate energy needs.[8]

[4] *SWB* MEW/0375 WME/3 14 March 1995.
[5] Calabrese, op. cit., p. 87.
[6] *Middle East Economic Digest*, 15 November 1990, p. 5, cited in Ramazani, op. cit., p. 404.
[7] *Kayhan International*, 29 September 1994.
[8] Associated Press, 8 May 1995.

Developments in trade with Azerbaijan have been scarcely less dramatic: Iran is currently Azerbaijan's major trade partner, but here too the Iranian advantage is artificial, created by the Russian blockade that was imposed with varying severity from autumn 1994. According to S. Sadykhov, Azerbaijan's vice-premier and minister of economics, imports from Iran stand at $66 million and exports at $242 million (39 per cent and 42 per cent of Azerbaijan's national totals).[9] According to the Iranian ambassador to Azerbaijan, trade turnover between the countries amounted to $500 million, constituting 60 per cent of Iran's trade with the CIS (Azerbaijan, therefore, now occupies the place held by Russia in 1992–3), while yet another authority puts trade with Iran at 21 per cent of Azerbaijan's foreign trade in the first 11 months of 1994.[10] In the event of the lifting of the several blockades, the inflated trade across Iran's northwestern border would shrink, at least in the short term, though its long-term prospects would improve if peace and stability opened the way for economic recovery in the region.[11] Trade with Turkmenistan has developed relatively smoothly and without similar distortions and has reached encouraging proportions. The trade agreements of March, May and July 1992 were on a significant scale, including a $50 million Iranian credit to allow Turkmenistan to import Iranian foodstuffs. The overall volume of trade between Iran and the FSS may still be fairly small, but the rate of growth of non-energy exports has been rapid (though starting from a very low threshold), which is a source of particular satisfaction to the Iranian government.[12]

A visible part in Iran's commercial relations with the FSS states is played by the Iranian petty traders. In Baku, Erevan and Ashgabat they have become very much a part of the local scene. The overall turnover of this trade is impossible to assess (it mainly goes unrecorded), but for those involved it offers a welcome escape from the employment and economic difficulties at home. It also generates contact between Iranians and the peoples of the FSS countries, though traditional popular attitudes towards traders are not always conducive to the formation of favourable impressions of Iran and Iranians.

Sub-national relations

A significant feature of the developing economic relations with neighbouring FSS countries is the partial devolution to provincial level, which also has interesting implications for the development of regional autonomy inside Iran.[13] The first signs of this

---

[9] FBIS-SOV-95-059, 28 March 1995.

[10] FBIS-NES-95-020, 31 January 1995; FBIS-SOV-95-039, 28 February 1995.

[11] *Nezavisimaya Gazeta*, 18 April 1995.

[12] *Kayhan International*, 29 September 1994.

[13] K.L. Afrasiabi, *After Khomeini: New Directions in Iran's Foreign Policy* (Boulder, CO: Westview Press, 1994), p. 128.

occurred in 1991, when agreements were reached on opening new border crossings with Azerbaijan and Turkmenistan for the use of residents of the border regions in Iran's West and East Azerbaijan and Mazandaran provinces. Since then there have been a number of further regional agreements involving these Iranian provinces, as well as Gilan and Khorasan, with Azerbaijan, Turkmenistan and Kazakhstan. The proposal for a free trade zone at Bandar Anzali apparently originated at negotiations between Gilan province and Azerbaijan, and contracts with Turkmenistan and Kazakhstan worth $40 million have been negotiated by Khorasani and Mazandarani businesses.[14] Gilan has also negotiated with Mangystau province (*oblast*) of Kazakhstan over closer economic links and the opening of a shipping line.[15]

Bilateral cooperation

Cooperation is a central plank of Iranian regional economic policy and has been the subject of frequent discussions and a large number of agreements. Perhaps the most significant initiatives have been at the multilateral levels with ECO and Caspian Sea cooperation (see below), but there has also been a determined drive at the bilateral level. Much of what has been discussed and agreed remains unfulfilled, but some joint ventures are operating and a number of joint projects are in progress or imminent (those in the pipelines, transport and communications sector are discussed in the relevant section below). In Azerbaijan, for example, there are seventy-eight joint ventures in the light engineering, light industrial, food and agricultural sectors, as well as a joint shipping company operating in the Caspian Sea. There are plans for fertilizer production and for an Iranian-built cement factory in Nakhichevan.[16]

The oil and gas sector is considered particularly suitable for cooperation in view of the rich resources of Iran and the FSS states and their complementary experiences in the industry and technical skills. Joint oil exploration, extraction and refining agreements have been signed with Azerbaijan, Kazakhstan and Turkmenistan. Iran has resumed oil exploration in the Caspian with Azerbaijani assistance and equipment, and plans to build an oil refinery in Nakhichevan.[17] Two jointly owned Iranian and Turkmen oil companies have been set up, one to prospect and drill, the other to trade Turkmen oil and its by-products from the National Iranian Oil Company Office in London.[18]

The establishment of free trade zones at access points around its borders is an established part of Iran's foreign economic policy. These zones serve the dual purpose

[14] Calabrese, op. cit., pp. 88, 95.
[15] FBIS-SOV-94-191, 3 October 1994.
[16] FBIS-SOV-95-059, 28 March 1995.
[17] FBIS-SOV-95-039, 28 February 1995.
[18] *SWB* SUW/0355 WD/4, 21 October 1994.

of encouraging and channelling foreign trade and investment and circumventing Iran's constitutional obstacles to foreign investment.[19] To date four free trade zones are proposed for Iran's northern frontiers: at Sarakhs, on the border with Turkmenistan, at Anzali on the Caspian, at Astara on the border with Azerbaijan and a fourth on the border with Nakhichevan. The Sarakhs free trade zone is already said to be playing a significant role in the developing economic relations between the countries.

ECO

The revitalization of the Economic Cooperation Organization (set up in 1985 as a successor to the Regional Cooperation for Development that had united Turkey, Iran and Pakistan) has been one of Iran's major objectives of the 1990s.[20] It was mainly on Iran's initiative that the moribund organization was expanded to include Afghanistan and the six 'Islamic' FSS states (Armenia's expression of interest in joining fell on deaf ears[21]) at its summit meeting in Tehran in February 1992.[22] There have been several subsequent high-level ECO meetings, and the organization has also featured in many of Iran's bilateral discussions with FSS states.

The principal concrete proposals put forward at ECO meetings have been for the formation of an ECO Trade and Development Bank (its headquarters will be in Istanbul and its first branches will open in Iran and Pakistan); coordination and development of member states' transport and communications links (one of Iran's favourite projects – see below); tariff reductions; an ECO reinsurance company; and cooperation in combating the drugs trade and organized crime. There has, however, been little in the way of actual progress. Iran's long-term objective is the creation of an Islamic common market to link the 300 million Muslims living between the Mediterranean Sea and the Indian Ocean. This goal is not only remote, but controversial as well; while other member states view ECO primarily as a vehicle for mutual economic coordination and cooperation, Iran has sought to widen its agenda to include cultural and religious affairs (joint positions on Bosnia, warnings against US domination, etc.). Moreover the possibility that Iran may wish for a future security dimension cannot be discounted (see Chapter 2). Iran has also sought to raise the organization's standing *vis-à-vis* other multilateral organizations (the Association of Southeast Asian Nations, the European Community, various UN agencies, the OIC, etc.). The belief that Iran is

[19] Calabrese, op. cit., pp. 94–5; Kh. Nur-Mohammadi, '*Ravabet-e eqtesadi-ye Jomhuriye Eslami-ye Iran ba keshvar-ha-ye Asiya-ye Markazi va Qafqaz* (The Islamic Republic of Iran's Economic Relations with the Countries of Central Asia and the Caucasus)', *MMAMQ*, vol. 3, no. 8 (1995), pp. 145–6.
[20] Calabrese, op. cit., pp. 95–8; Afrasiabi, op. cit., pp. 120–5.
[21] FBIS-NES-92-027, 10 February 1992.
[22] FBIS-NES-92-032, 18 February 1992.

trying to use ECO as a platform for its own ideological ambitions and to enhance its international profile has engendered disillusion in some of the other members. There are also anxieties about the organization's ability to convert words to action. As none of the members is currently in a position to support the kind of investment required for the more grandiose schemes, such anxieties seem well founded. Rivalry, both among the main members and with other multilateral groupings – the CIS, the Black and Caspian Sea Cooperation, and the several nascent Eurasian and Central Asian groupings – also have the potential to drain ECO's vitality.[23]

If it is unlikely that ECO will become an effective economic force in the near future, it can still serve a useful function for Iran and the other member states by providing a forum for the discussion of issues of mutual interest and concern, and as a vehicle for raising their international profile. In this sense, Iran's exploitation of the organization's extra-economic potential, if it is not excessively ideological, appears sensible and potentially effective. Certainly the rejuvenation and expansion of ECO should be considered a foreign policy success for Iran.

Caspian Sea cooperation

Another important focus of Iranian initiatives for multilateral cooperation with the FSS is the promotion of dialogue among the five states surrounding the Caspian Sea: Iran, Azerbaijan, Russia, Kazakhstan and Turkmenistan. When the idea of a Caspian Sea Cooperation Organization and a treaty on regional cooperation by the Caspian states was mooted by Akbar Hashemi-Rafsanjani during the February 1992 ECO conference in Tehran, it was widely dismissed as a spoiling operation to compete with Turkey's Black Sea Cooperation.[24] In fact a standing Caspian Sea Cooperation Organization, with a permanent headquarters and staff, is still to be established, but any inclination to write the initiative off as an Iranian propaganda exercise must be reconsidered in view both of the relatively strong support shown by the other littoral states, and of the numerous issues connected with the Caspian Sea that can be resolved only through agreement among the littoral states. These issues were suddenly brought to the world's attention at the end of September 1994 by the signature of the 'contract of the century' – the deal between Azerbaijan and a consortium of mainly Western oil companies for the exploitation of three oilfields off the coast of Azerbaijan.

Between February 1992 and September 1994 the record of activity and achievement of Caspian Sea cooperation was rather impressive. A five-day conference was

[23] Afrasiabi, loc. cit.; *Moscow News*, 23 July 1993; FBIS-NES-94-189, 29 September 1994; *Aziya i Afrika segodnya*, no. 11 (1994), p. 36; *Transition*, vol. 1, no. 6 (28 April 1995), p. 43.

[24] For reactions to the Iranian proposal, see A. Saville and P. Mosteshar in *The Independent*, 18 February 1992; P. Feuilherade in *The Guardian*, 14 February 1992.

held in April 1992 which came to general agreements on Caspian environmental protection, navigation and passenger traffic, as well as reaching concrete agreements to establish a shipping line to link Iran and Turkmenistan, and to open Kazakhstan's port of Shevchenko (now Aktau) to Iranian exports for transit to the Far East. In October of the same year, at a meeting in Tehran, the five littoral states agreed to form six committees with responsibility for the legal status of the Caspian, environmental protection, conservation and exploitation of biological resources (fish stocks), prospecting for and exploiting mineral resources (including oil and gas), shipping and ports, and marine research (including the study of the causes of the variations in the sea's level). The next month Russia and Iran agreed to establish a joint research centre for Caspian Sea studies. Caspian Sea cooperation was on the agenda for discussions during the visits of the Azerbaijani vice-president in December 1992 and the Russian foreign minister, Andrei Kozyrev, to Teheran in March 1993. In February 1993 a joint Azerbaijani and Iranian shipping company started a twice-weekly ferry service between Baku and Anzali. In June of that year there were further discussions about setting up a Caspian Sea research centre and it was announced that the other three littoral states would join Russia and Iran in the project. In August the Caspian states met in Anzali and agreed to coordinate the caviar trade. In November Iran announced that it would build a new port at Fereidun Kenar to serve the growing cooperation between Caspian states. In June 1994 a delegation from Kazakhstan's Mangystau province (*oblast*) visited Gilan and Mazandaran (Iran's two Caspian provinces) and signed a number of agreements.

These promising beginnings notwithstanding, since the signing of the September 1994 Baku contract, the frequently expressed hope that the Caspian should be a sea of friendship and cooperation has sounded decidedly hollow. Azerbaijan and Russia (to be precise the Russian foreign ministry) are locked in a dispute about the legality of the contract and the status of the Caspian (for Iran's position in the dispute, see below). This dispute has inevitably had a negative impact on Caspian cooperation, though there have been further meetings of the five Caspian states, in Moscow in October 1994, at which they reiterated the need for a coordinated approach to the problems of the sea and drafted an agreement on cooperation (based on the 1992 Iranian proposal) that envisaged the establishment of a five-nation Caspian Sea Cooperation Organization. The participants also agreed on the need for early discussions on the legal status of the Caspian. In March 1995, following a visit to Iran by a Russian parliamentary delegation, Iran announced the hope that there would be an interparliamentary meeting of the five littoral states before the end of the year. In May 1995 a conference of the Caspian states was held in Almaty (though Turkmenistan did not send a delegation), but this revealed the outstanding differences between the states rather than bringing them closer together.

Iran's interests and concerns in relation to the Caspian Sea can be divided into two broad categories: those that are related to the sea itself and those that have a broader regional character.[25] In the latter category are similar interests to those informing Iran's general FSS policies: enhancing regional status, excluding hostile forces and escaping isolation, taking advantage of the new opportunities to enhance its geo-economic role as a transit centre, and so on.

There are a number of interests relating directly to the Caspian.

(1) Iran wishes to improve its position *vis-à-vis* the other littoral states. During the Tsarist and Soviet periods the Caspian was effectively a Russian-Soviet lake. Iran hopes to establish a better place for itself in the post-Soviet Caspian.

(2) The rising level of the Caspian (three metres since 1977) has affected Iran more seriously than the other states, flooding large areas of its coastal plain. Iran would like to see cooperation to study the problem and discover a solution.

(3) The sea is already badly polluted by the Soviet-era oil and other industries. Iran is concerned about the threat to the sea's ecosystem and to marine resources, on which a part of its coastal population depends. It believes that regulation and concerted action are required to tackle this problem.

(4) Iran is interested in developing its own Caspian energy resources, in cooperation with its neighbours, and in participating in their Caspian oil and gas industries.

(5) Iran is keen to develop Caspian shipping and port facilities to bring it closer to its littoral neighbours and to contribute to its ambitions as a transit centre (see below).

(6) Iran would like to be the chosen route for at least some of the oil and gas exports from the Caspian.

(7) Iran has no naval presence on the Caspian and sees the break-up of the Soviet Caspian fleet among the other states as a security threat. It would like the sea to be demilitarized.

On the crucial question of the Caspian Sea's legal status,[26] Iran's position is to favour the idea of a condominium or joint sovereignty regime. This is justified on the

---

[25] The fullest published account of Iran's view of the Caspian Sea is M.-R. Dabiri's 'A New Approach to the Legal Regime of the Caspian Sea as a Basis for Peace and Development', which has been published both in *The Iranian Journal of International Affairs*, vol. 6, nos. 1–2 (1994), pp. 28–46, and in *Kayhan International*, 29 September 1994 (also in Persian in *MMAMQ*, vol. 3, no. 5 (1994), pp. 1–20). Although the article does not represent an official position, Dr Dabiri is Deputy Director-General for Research at Iran's Foreign Ministry Institute for Political and International Studies, and his views conform to official statements on the Caspian.

[26] H.-J. Uibopuu, 'The Caspian Sea: a Tangle of Legal Problems', *The World Today*, vol. 51, no. 6, June 1995, pp. 119–23.

basis of an interpretation of the Irano–Soviet treaties of 1921 and 1940 which did not delimit a border between Iranian and Soviet sectors of the sea, and which spoke of an 'Iran-Soviet sea'. Such a regime would serve Iran's interests well, suggesting some form of joint ownership of the sea's resources and a veto for individual states on foreign participation in Caspian projects. It should be noted, however, that while Iran has claimed that this regime is currently in effect, it has not insisted on its final adoption as the basis for the new legal regime; instead it has emphasized that the current uncertain status is an impediment to the mutually advantageous exploitation of the sea's resources and a source of instability and tension. It has urged that the question be resolved by mutual agreement as soon as possible.

The 'contract of the century'

Iran's position towards the Azerbaijani oil contract of September 1994 was particularly revealing of Tehran's policies and priorities. When the contract was signed Iran did not protest, though the Russian foreign ministry's objections were based on a very similar understanding of the Caspian Sea legal issue to that held by Iran. There was some negative comment in the Iranian media about the penetration of Western multinationals into the region, but the Iranian ambassador to Azerbaijan denied allegations that Iran would cooperate with Russia against Azerbaijan's contract. In November Iran accepted a quarter of Azerbaijan's 20 per cent share in the consortium in return for $300–350 million, to be paid by supplying electricity and building an oil pipeline and refinery for Nakhichevan. Iran's entry into the consortium, in spite of its own understanding of the Caspian legal question and the Russian foreign ministry's objections to the contract, indicates the importance it attaches to relations with Azerbaijan, its desire to participate in regional economic development and to rebuff American attempts to exclude it; presumably a desire for profit also played a part. In April 1995, however, Iran was cut out of the consortium following US government pressure. Azerbaijan attempted to compensate by offering a share in another Caspian oil project (Shakh Deniz), which does not involve US companies, but Iran was clearly aggrieved. The humiliating rejection confirmed all its worst fears about the sinister nature of Western economic penetration into the region and will strengthen the hand of Tehran's hardliners, who are determined to keep foreign companies and investment out of Iran. Particularly galling to Iran was Baku's willingness to allow Washington to dictate the terms for the exploitation of Azerbaijan's resources – a surrender of sovereignty that rankled all the more in the light of the frequent accusations in the Azerbaijani media that Russia and Iran are seeking to undermine Azerbaijan's sovereignty. Tehran reacted by reasserting its own original position that the 1921 and 1940 treaties implied joint sovereignty and, therefore, that all littoral states must agree to any offshore development. Even so the message, delivered by the deputy foreign minister, Abbas Maleki, at the May 1995 Almaty conference, remained much milder than the Russian foreign ministry's and stopped short of declaring the contract invalid: 'We want to compromise with all the countries. But until there is a new legal regime, the old regime is in effect.'[27]

The central questions regarding the Caspian Sea's legal status and the best basis for exploiting its energy resources remain unresolved, but this fact tends to confirm the high priority that Iran attaches to the idea of Caspian Sea cooperation. Apart from its humiliation over the Azerbaijan oil contract, Iran's Caspian Sea diplomacy can be viewed as a success. If cooperation and agreement have proved hard to attain, it is because of genuine differences of interest and perception between the Caspian states, as well as the quite specific legal, economic and ecological problems arising from the break-up of the Soviet Union; it is not because the idea of a Caspian Sea Cooperation Organization is badly conceived. In contrast to the ECO initiative, Tehran has resisted the temptation to widen the issues or use the Caspian grouping as an international platform.

Transport and communications

The dream of revitalizing the ancient silk road with Iran and the FSS at its heart has a powerful appeal in the region. In part that appeal is romantic – it harks back to a time of economic prosperity, political power and cultural glory, when this was the meeting-point of the world's great civilizations. More mundanely, it also harmonizes with Iran's desire to reintegrate itself with its neighbours and the international community and to enhance its status. Projecting itself as the future geo-economic centre for a vast new transit system helps to offset its current isolation. The development of transport and communications links with the FSS could also produce some significant economic benefits, in terms of stimulating trade and transport services and in transit charges.[28] In an interview during the 1992 ECO summit in Tehran, Akbar Hashemi-Rafsanjani revealed the extent of Iran's ambitions:

> As you can see on the map, Iran links the ECO member states with one another. Cooperation should be certainly carried out via Iran. For links between the north and the south, the east and the west, these countries and Europe, Europe and Asia, everything

---

[27] *The Financial Times*, 17 May 1995.

[28] Calabrese, op. cit., pp. 91–5; G. McDonell, *The Euro-Asian Corridor: Freight and Energy Transport for Central Asia and the Caspian Region* (London: RIIA, Post-Soviet Business Forum, 1995); A. Kazemi, '*Tause'eh va mas'aleh-ye tranzit-e keshvar-ha-ye Asiya-ye Markazi va Qafqaz* (Development and the Transit Question in the Countries of Central Asia and the Caucasus)', *MMAMQ*, vol. 2, no. 4 (1994), pp. 91–108.

should cross Iran – oil and gas pipelines, railways, communication routes and international airports.[29]

Iranian leaders have been promoting this vision with considerable eloquence and enthusiasm, and have received quite a favourable response at international forums such as ECO; the project for transit links via Iran to the Persian Gulf attracts all the Central Asian leaders, and appears to be the aspect of relations with Iran that most appeals to President Islam Karimov of Uzbekistan. The dream's realization, however, remains extremely remote; Iran's and ECO's lack of investment capital, and the current obstacles to raising Western and international assistance because of American opposition to any project involving Iran, mean that for the moment there can be only very slow progress. Nevertheless, transport and communications have figured prominently in Iran's diplomatic contacts with the FSS states and in their agreements (see Chapter 3). As well as broad commitments to transport cooperation, Iran and its provinces have established direct air services with all the FSS states.

Some of the obstacles to communication with the FSS relate to the deliberate minimization of access during the Soviet period. The opening of new border crossings, the construction of bridges, the development of road, rail and telecommunications infrastructure in the vicinity of borders, and the opening of Caspian ports and shipping lines (see above) go some way to overcoming this barrier and can be achieved at relatively little cost. Several new border crossings have opened with Nakhichevan, Armenia, Azerbaijan and Turkmenistan, though a number of them give only very restricted access. Bridges (some only temporary) have been opened on the border with Armenia, at Khoda-Afarin on the Azerbaijani border and on the Turkmen border. Agreement has been reached to establish direct telecommunications links with Azerbaijan and Turkmenistan (and through them with other CIS states), and Iran has agreed to build a cable network in Turkmenistan.

Iran's only rail link with the Soviet Union was through Julfa in Nakhichevan. The Armenian blockade means that even this link has been severed. Agreement has been reached on building new links between the Iranian railway network and Azerbaijan and Turkmenistan. On the Azerbaijani side the railway track already extends as far as the border at Astara, but it is over 150 kilometres from there to the closest point on the Iranian railway network on the line linking Tehran with Tabriz via Zanjan. So far this link is only at the planning stage. The connection with Turkmenistan, which was originally agreed in the Soviet era (see Chapter 1) is further advanced, however: the Turkmen line linking Tedzhen and Sarakhs has been completed and the 170-kilometre Iranian track between Mashhad and Sarakhs is due to be completed in 1995. Iran has not

[29] Cited in Calabrese, op. cit., p. 80.

found it easy to raise the capital for even this fairly modest line and the break-of-gauge connection and terminal at the border are still to be built.[30]

Iran's major rail project, however, is for a direct line linking Central Asia (via Turkmenistan) and the Caspian (at the planned new port of Fereidun Kenar near Sari, or at Bandar-e Torkeman, which already has a rail link) with the Persian Gulf port Bandar Abbas. The most important section to be constructed is that between Bandar Abbas and Bafq, which requires about 500 kilometres of track. This would give Turkmenistan and through it Uzbekistan, Kazakhstan, Russia and China railway access to the Persian Gulf. President Akbar Hashemi-Rafsanjani inaugurated the line in March 1995, but it is far from certain that Iran and ECO will be able to raise the investment needed for its construction.

Rail links have been given the highest profile in Iran's plans for new transit routes, but roads also have a place. A number of plans and proposals have been put forward and accepted, but no major projects have as yet been completed.

Oil and gas pipelines

Iran's ambitions for a share in the transport of the region's oil and gas resources are no less ambitious than its plans for railways and roads. Agreements have been reached for various pipeline projects with Nakhichevan, Armenia, Azerbaijan, Georgia, Russia and Ukraine. It is unlikely that any but a few of these projects will ever be realized. It now also appears almost certain that Iran will not be the route chosen for a major pipeline serving the new Azerbaijani oil development. Iran offered a possible route either by connecting with its own pipeline infrastructure to the Persian Gulf, or as a way round Armenia to link Azerbaijan with Nakhichevan and Turkey. The reason for the rejection of an Iranian route is not economic (some experts prefer this option) but political: US objections. Iran is, however, likely to be involved in the export of 'early oil' from the fields through swap arrangements (it has also made swap agreements with Kazakhstan). The great advantage of these for Iran is that its own oilfields are located in the south of the country, from where the oil can easily be shipped out via the Persian Gulf, but the main demand is in the more populous north. Swapping oil and gas with nearby FSS countries can serve Iranian demand and release oil and gas for export in the south.

Much the most significant development in this field, however, is the agreement, signed in Tehran in August 1994 in the presence of representatives from Turkey, Russia and Kazakhstan, to build a pipeline to carry gas from Turkmenistan to Europe. Turkmenistan's interest in the project was spurred by its difficulties in getting its gas

---

[30] McDonell, op. cit., pp. 11–13.

to world markets via the existing CIS network. The project is on a very large scale, the total cost being estimated at between $5 and $7 billion, with the Iranian section costing perhaps $3.5 billion.[31] While some experts consider the project viable in economic terms, its financing must be in doubt because of US objections, if for no other reason, while some are sceptical about the possibility of achieving the necessary cooperation along the string of states between Turkmenistan and the eventual European markets.

Iran's hopes of becoming a major geo-economic power through its position at the heart of a new network of road, rail, pipeline and telecommunications links has been a major motivating factor in its desire for closer relations with the FSS states. It also serves an important rhetorical function, helping Iran to project an image of itself as central to the FSS region's economic development and global orientation. So far, however, progress has been slow. Massive investment will be needed to create the infrastructure required for Iran to become an effective bridge between the region and the world, and currently it is hard to see how Iran will find investment on such a scale. In terms of the more limited goal of building the necessary links to support its own economic relations with the FSS countries, however, the prospects are brighter, and this will in itself generate considerable benefits for Iran and for its northern border provinces. Iranian businesses, engineers, technicians and entrepreneurs, starved of the investment required to galvanize the national economy into recovery, may be able to garner worthwhile fringe benefits from the anticipated international investments in the FSS economies.

---

[31] *The Financial Times*, 24, 26 August 1994.

5 CULTURE AND RELIGION

The West tends to associate contemporary Iran exclusively with the ideology of Islamic revolution and a severe and narrow Islamic culture that rejects not only Western values and culture, but almost anything that does not have an explicit Islamic content. This image seriously distorts the ideological and cultural policies and character of the Islamic Republic, which have grown progressively broader and more inclusive as time goes on. This is not to suggest that the austere and radical elements of contemporary Islam have been rejected or even diluted, but rather to point out that there has been a growing recognition of the continuing vitality and appeal (to national pride as much as to national taste) of many other aspects of Islamic Persian culture. Classical Persian music, painting and most of all literature are all vigorously promoted in today's Islamic Republic, though of course the Islamic element in classical Persian culture is emphasized now, just as the national aspects were in the Pahlavi period. There can be no doubt that the Iranian government (following a lead given by Ayatollah Khomeini) has adopted a deliberate policy of broadening the definition of what constitutes acceptable Islamic culture. Culture is a controversial issue within the Iranian leadership, as the recent controversy over TV satellite dishes has illustrated, but in this field, as in others, the pragmatists have been making slow, if not steady, headway against the objections of the hardliners for most of the past decade. One aspect of this cultural policy is the reclamation for the Islamic Republic of cultural monuments that were mobilized to support the monarchical nationalist ideology of the previous government. To cite one significant example, at a major international conference in Tehran in 1990, the *Shahnameh* (*Book of Kings*) of Ferdausi was publicly rehabilitated as a masterpiece of Islamic Persian literature, although it had been viewed with suspicion and antipathy by many supporters of the revolution because of its earlier 'rediscovery' and promotion by twentieth-century Iranian nationalists and the Pahlavi government as a text glorifying Iran's pre-Islamic monarchical past.

From one perspective this may be viewed as the cynical manipulation of culture by the current government in an attempt to broaden its appeal. From another it may be considered a natural historical evolution, as the cultural policy of the Iranian revolutionary state grows increasingly conservative and inclusive as that state seeks to consolidate its legitimacy and achieve a national consensus of support. At least in part, the process is part of a continuing broad national debate about the culture and identity of contemporary Iranian society.

This development in Iranian domestic cultural policy has had an impact on foreign policy. While the ideological support for Islamic resistance to Western imperialism and its lackeys still has its place, particularly in relations with the Arab world and with minority Muslim causes (such as Kashmir and Bosnia), Tehran also now emphasizes Islam as a unifying force for Muslim states, helping them to cooperate with one another and develop common policies and approaches. In its relations with those countries that share the heritage of Islamic Persian civilization – Turkey, the 'Muslim' FSS states, Afghanistan, Pakistan and India – Iran increasingly also emphasizes the unifying and supranational characteristics of that heritage. This conception of a revived eastern Islamic world (roughly the same shape as in the pre-modern period, and with Iran at its heart) is what lies behind Iran's hopes for an Islamic common market embodied in ECO. If Iran does not actually attempt to promote cooperation with these countries on the basis of radical Islam, it is quite possible that in the future it will mobilize that cooperation to promote radical Islam.

Projecting an image to the FSS states

The previous chapters have argued that the Iranian government perceives its interests in the FSS region as being in enhancing regional stability, discouraging unfriendly penetration, developing neighbourly relations and economic cooperation, and maintaining good relations with Russia. In the light of this, it is scarcely surprising that in its cultural relations with the FSS states Iran has emphasized Islamic unity and the shared heritage of Persian civilization, rather than radical Islam.[1] This marks a significant departure from the Soviet era, when the Islamic Republic broadcast radical Islamic propaganda to the Soviet south. Today's broadcasting is still Islamic, but much less incendiary.

When Akbar Hashemi-Rafsanjani said in 1992 that the Islamic Republic of Iran offered an 'ideal model' for the 'Muslim' FSS states, he was not urging their populations to Islamic revolution against their secular governments, nor was he suggesting that these states should adopt Iran's constitution or the distinct, and distinctively Shi'i, concept of Islamic government developed by Ayatollah Khomeini. What he was promoting was the idea of Islam as a supranational spiritual force capable of bringing Muslims together at the national level (as in Iran's multi-ethnic state) and internation-

---

[1] K.L. Afrasiabi, *After Khomeini: New Directions in Iran's Foreign Policy* (Boulder, CO: Westview Press, 1994), pp. 132–40.

ally through interstate cooperation both bilaterally and through regional and international organizations (a message that Iran's representatives continually broadcast at the OIC and other forums).[2]

More generally, the image Iran presents to the FSS countries is one of a state committed to the principles of respect for sovereignty, territorial integrity, and non-interference in another state's internal affairs; a state looking for friendly cooperative relations in the political, economic and cultural spheres. There may not appear to be anything particularly Islamic about these characteristics, but in the eyes of Iran's leaders, they spring from basic Islamic values. It is not difficult to identify inconsistencies in the professed desire for friendly cooperative relations and Tehran's evident aspirations for leadership, both as a regional power and as an Islamic vanguard state. The contradiction between this message and the one Tehran communicates to radical Islamic organizations in the Arab world is even more glaring. In Tehran's eyes, however, there is no contradiction in the message, which is always Islam, but there are differing tactical responses appropriate to a variety of situations.

Persian civilization and the former Soviet South

The Caucasus and Central Asia, particularly the latter, occupy an important place in the historical geography of Persian civilization. Much of the region was included in the pre-Islamic Persian empires, and many of its ancient peoples either belonged to the Iranian branch of the Indo-European peoples (e.g. the Medes and Soghdians) or were in close cultural contact with them (e.g. the Armenians).

In the centuries following the Islamic conquest of the eighth century, most of the peoples of the Caucasus and Central Asia (with the important exceptions of the Georgians and Armenians) became Muslim, and much of the region (though not the territory of present-day Kazakhstan and Kyrgyzstan) was incorporated into the early Islamic empire, the caliphate. By about the tenth century the caliphate began to fragment, with provincial governors asserting increasing autonomy and eventual independence from the capital, Baghdad. It was at the courts of such governors, later princes and kings, in the northeastern territories of the caliphate (present-day northeast Iran, northwest Afghanistan, Turkmenistan and Uzbekistan) that the new Persian language emerged. A crucial early role in this process was played by the courts of the Samani and Ghaznavi dynasties in Bukhara and Samarqand (now in Uzbekistan), and Ghazna (now in Afghanistan), which provided the patronage for the first new Persian poets, among them the founding fathers of classical Persian literature, Rudaki and Ferdausi.

---

[2] Again it is interesting to note that Ayatollah Khomeini's letter to Mikhail Gorbachev emphasized Islam as a spiritual, not a political, force and recommended several medieval Islamic philosophers and mystics (not modern Islamic radicals).

Another contemporary development was the entry into the Islamic world of increasing numbers of Turkish peoples, originally pastoral nomads from the Eurasian steppe. They rapidly established themselves as the principal source of military manpower and not long after achieved a virtual monopoly of political power in the eastern Islamic world. This situation persisted until the nineteenth or even twentieth centuries, when European colonialism and emerging nationalist political forces at last dislodged the Turkish dynasties that had for so long dominated the area between Istanbul and Bengal.

These Turkish dynasties provided much of the patronage for the flowering of Persian literature and the other arts of medieval Islamic Persian civilization (including architecture, calligraphy and book painting), and carried that civilization with them to Anatolia and India, where it enjoyed high prestige in courtly and educated circles and exerted a powerful influence on the development of indigenous Islamic languages and cultures (Ottoman and Urdu).

The appeal of this medieval eastern Islamic civilization, whose principal vehicle was the Persian language, was not national (much less nationalist). It transcended political, ethnic, linguistic and religious frontiers, which were in any case more porous than in the modern world. Persian was not the first language of a great many of its admirers and practitioners. Turks made an enormous active contribution to Persian literature and other arts (in addition to providing patronage), just as Iranians made a great contribution to Islamic literature, scholarship and science through the medium of Arabic.

It is this shared Islamic Persian civilization which, from an Iranian perspective, provides the historical background and justification for the restoration of close cultural links with Azerbaijan and the Central Asian states (particularly Turkmenistan, Tajikistan and Uzbekistan). Iranian leaders emphasize that Persian Islamic culture can help these countries develop friendly relations, facilitate mutual understanding and contribute to regional stability and harmony. Iran sees a unique role for itself in this process of renewing cultural affiliation, both because it is the largest Persian-speaking country and therefore the natural contemporary bearer of Persian culture, and because Persian literature and culture have enjoyed uninterrupted prestige, appreciation, study and encouragement in Iran, whereas in the FSS, according to the prevalent Iranian opinion, the Muslim peoples were deliberately deprived of their culture and religion and artificially separated from their Middle Eastern cultural and spiritual brethren by Russian imperialism and Soviet Marxism. It is in this sense that Ali Akbar Velayati spoke of the Islamic Republic's 'capacity to fill the intellectual vacuums and cultural needs' of the new states.[3]

---

[3] Cited in Afrasiabi, op. cit., p. 117.

The idea that the FSS is an Islamic 'sleeping beauty' awaiting the revivifying kiss of her Persian prince is a serious distortion of the region's cultural development under Russian and Soviet rule. While it is true that most ordinary Muslims in the FSS have only the most rudimentary knowledge of Islam and of their pre-modern literatures and cultures, this is not to say that they live in a cultural vacuum. During the Soviet period, secular Western and Russian culture came to be the dominant element in the cultural orientation of the educated urban elite, while at the same time a deliberate process of nationalization was applied to the histories and pre-modern cultures of all the Soviet peoples. This process, which formed part of the larger project of Soviet nation-building in the context of the republican system of the USSR, achieved a high degree of success in many republics. The result was the growth of new or reinforced national cultures among the titular nationalities of the fifteen union republics.[4]

Conversely, the Iranian conceptualization of classical Persian civilization and the notion that Iran is the rightful principal heir to that heritage stems in large part from the ideas of twentieth century Iranian nationalist intellectuals. In this respect the Islamic Republic is still carrying the cultural baggage of the Pahlavi period. Iranians take a justifiable pride in the richness of their cultural heritage, but it is significant that this consciousness of the value of Persian culture is closely associated with their sense of Iranian identity and their Iranian patriotism. Cultural nationalism retains a powerful attraction for many Iranian intellectuals, who often see themselves as representatives of a great historic civilization superior to that of their Middle Eastern neighbours, the Arabs and the Turks. In looking at their cultural history, they tend to play down the part of Turks and other non-Iranians in classical Persian civilization, often presenting them as barbarians assimilated by the sophisticated Persian culture. This nationalism also informs Iranian interpretations of the history of the region, which tend to project a greater Iran, at least in cultural terms, onto Azerbaijan and Central Asia. As was noted above (Chapter 3), Azerbaijani, Uzbek and other Central Asian claims to their independent national histories, cultures and even ethnicities are often rejected by Iranians as artificial or spurious. It is not hard to understand why Iranians ridicule claims such as Azerbaijan's to the Persian poet Nizami Ganjavi, or Uzbekistan's to the great Ibn Sina (Avicenna) – Ibn Sina would not even have known what an Uzbek was, let alone recognized the concept of Uzbekistan – but they tend to be less aware of the irony of their own claim to a privileged *national* role as first among equals among the heirs to Islamic Persian civilization, especially when they simultaneously promote that culture as an *international* heritage capable of cementing regional

---

[4] R.G. Suny, *The Revenge of the Past: Nationalism, Revolution and the Collapse of the Soviet Union* (Stanford, CA: Stanford University Press, 1993).

relations. Ultimately, all national claims to that heritage are anachronistic and alien to the spirit of a civilization that was unaware of the modern concept of nationality.

Viewed in this light, it is not surprising that Iran's cultural policy towards the FSS states has encountered obstacles. Only secular nationalist Tajik intellectuals have an understanding of their past history and culture that harmonizes closely with that of Iranians.[5] All the other 'Muslim' FSS republics are Turkic and generally subscribe either to their own nationalist interpretations of their past, or to some form of pan-Turkism, or to the idea of a distinct Turanian-Turkestani history and identity. All of these are incompatible with the Iranian interpretation.

The development of cultural relations

A survey of bilateral cultural relations reveals Iran's cultural priorities in the FSS. Tehran's cultural diplomacy has concentrated on the 'Muslim' states – culture has not played a major role in relations with Georgia and Armenia – and on Azerbaijan and Tajikistan in particular. Cultural and educational cooperation has featured in many of the bilateral negotiations and agreements. Iran offered to help Tajikistan change from the Cyrillic to the Arabic alphabet and has provided school textbooks. Iran offered scholarships to a number of Tajik students and agreed to establish a cultural centre and a technical university, though the civil war interrupted these initiatives. The Ministry of Islamic Guidance opened a branch of its al-Hoda bookshop chain in Dushanbe. In 1992 Iran also launched two initiatives to promote the Persian language internationally. One, the Association of Persian-speaking Countries, linked Iran, Afghanistan and Tajikistan; the other, which aimed at the global promotion of the Persian language, had Tajikistan and the Persian literary heritage of the FSS very much in mind. In the other Central Asian states Iran has achieved a much more limited degree of cultural influence and involvement. Many cultural agreements have been signed and there is a degree of educational and cultural exchange, including Iranian radio and television broadcasting, but the level of active cultural interaction remains relatively low.

Azerbaijan is the only FSS state where the majority of the population adhere to the same branch of Shi'i Islam as most Iranians. This, as well as the large Azerbaijani minority in Iran, has greatly facilitated the growth of cultural relations at the grass-roots as well as the official level. In general those relations have had a rather recipro-

---

[5] Even among the Tajiks there is scope for discord, as some Tajik nationalists subscribe to the idea of a historic greater Khorasan, in which their forebears played the leading role in developing Persian literature and culture, which was subsequently assimilated by the Iranians of the Iranian plateau (the ancestors of most contemporary Iranians).

cal character: Azerbaijan has made a small opening for Iranian religious activity in exchange for greater access to Azerbaijani language and culture for Azerbaijanis in Iran. Iran has welcomed Azerbaijani pilgrims to its shrines and has attempted to forge links with Azerbaijani clerics. Agreement has also been reached on radio and television broadcasting. In addition, Iran has had the opportunity to spread its cultural and religious influence among the Azerbaijani refugees in the camps it set up in the aftermath of the Armenian offensive of summer 1993.

Iran and militant Islam in the FSS

Interest in spreading radical political Islam has been conspicuous by its absence from Iranian pronouncements on its cultural relations with the FSS states. It has been argued above that the government of the Islamic Republic, and certainly its presidency and foreign ministry, see all forms of instability in the region as inimical to Iran's interests and have shaped their cultural policy accordingly. The progress of cultural relations to date seems to conform to this pattern. In Tajikistan the emphasis in relations has been on language and literature and has been mediated primarily by intellectuals and artists, rather than by clerics and Islamic activists. This may to some extent be attributable to the fact that Tajikistan's Islamic opposition is Sunni and looks for support to Afghanistan, Pakistan and Saudi Arabia, rather than Iran; but even in 'Shi'i' Azerbaijan, where there might be greater scope for Iranian religious activity, Iran seems to have focused on assisting in Azerbaijan's spiritual revival through legitimate channels, rather than on inciting Islamic revolution or opposition. Even this level of religious participation is sufficient to worry many secular Azerbaijanis. Iranian Islamic foundations are active in Azerbaijan and Central Asia, but their activities to date seem to have been mainly in the humanitarian field (such as supporting war refugees). Iran also contributed to the wave of mosque-building that has swept Central Asia, and to the propagation of Islam through publications, but in these areas it has played a relatively small role by comparison with other Islamic countries, notably Saudi Arabia.

The possibility that Iran is running a covert parallel radical religious foreign policy cannot be ruled out,[6] and it is entirely plausible that there may be agencies in Iran that would like to promote a radical Islamic policy in the FSS, probably as much to discredit the current pragmatist policies and leadership as for its own sake, but there is little if any credible evidence of Iranian propaganda for radical Islam and support for Islamic political opposition. There have been accusations from the Mojahedin-e Khalq and some Azerbaijani secular nationalists that Iran is training missionaries and revolutionaries to send to the region, but these cannot be considered reliable sources.

---

[6] Reliable information about developments at grass-roots level in the FSS is still not readily accessible.

Apart from the Iranian government's disinclination towards spreading a revolutionary message in the FSS, there are specific obstacles to Iran achieving significant religious influence in the region: the strong secular traditions of the educated elites of these countries; the suspicion of Iranian hegemonic ambitions, particularly among the Turkic peoples; and the incompatibility of the various manifestations of Islam in the FSS with Iran's clerically-dominated, non-Sufi Twelver Shi'ism. Even Islamic radicals do not look to the Islamic Republic of Iran for leadership; they seem to be unimpressed by Iran as a model for an Islamic society and to favour other radical Islamic thinkers over Ayatollah Khomeini. Islamic revival in the FSS, in both its mainstream and radical manifestations, seems to be primarily a home-grown phenomenon. In so far as FSS Muslims do look for external support, they seem to be more receptive to influence from Afghan Mojahedin groups, Arab and Turkish Islamists, the Naqshbandi Sufi order, Pakistan and Saudi Arabia than from Iran.[7]

Even so, the possibility of future Iranian backing for a radical political Islamic movement in the FSS cannot be excluded. The preconditions for the development of such a movement are already present: severe socio-economic pressures are already leading to the breakdown of traditional social structures and values, and among the losers in the current period of rapid change, disillusion with Western ideologies, both Soviet-Marxist and capitalist-democratic, is already spreading. Radical Islam, with its utopian vision of a just society and its uncompromising rejection of the West's materialist culture, is likely to hold a strong appeal for the new alienated underclass. It is hard to predict the response of a future Iranian government to the emergence of an Islamic mass movement in one of the FSS countries, or to an appeal from an Islamic group suffering repression from an authoritarian secular government. The broadcasting agreements, the growing direct links and ease of travel, and the presence of Iranian Islamic foundations in FSS countries certainly give the Islamic Republic a much enhanced capacity to communicate its message to the peoples of the FSS. In the short term, however, the refusal to back the Tajik opposition gives a clear indication of Tehran's current priorities.

On the broadest level, the revival of Islam in the FSS benefits Iran, irrespective of whether it is home-grown or sponsored by Iran's rivals in the Islamic world. The more 'Islamic' the FSS states and societies become, the easier it will be for Iran to emphasize Islam as the basis for relations and to promote its own regional status as a leading Islamic state.

---

[7] On Islam in the FSS, see M. Brill Olcott, 'Islam and Fundamentalism in Independent Central Asia', in Y. Ro'i (ed.), *Muslim Eurasia: Conflicting Legacies* (London: Frank Cass, the Cummings Centre Series, 1995), pp. 21–39; M. Haghayeghi, *Islam and Politics in Central Asia* (New York: St Martin's Press, 1995).

6 CONCLUSION

The preceding chapters have suggested an interpretation of Iranian interests in and policy towards the FSS that is based on official statements and speeches, analyses in official or semi-official publications and the record of developing relations. The picture that emerges is generally consistent over the whole range of issues involved and for the entire period since the onset of the Soviet collapse. In contrast to certain other areas of foreign policy, relations with the FSS have not become a controversial issue in Iran's internal political debate. Iranian policies and initiatives have encountered some setbacks, and ambitions have had to be scaled down, but there has been little change in the underlying analysis of the implications for Iran of the disintegration of the USSR, or in the basic principles and objectives of Iranian foreign policy towards the region.

To recapitulate the main strands of that policy:

(1) The opening up of a new group of neighbouring states has presented Iran with an opportunity to pursue its goals of reintegration into the international community, active regional cooperation to counter US global domination and the enhancement of its own status as a regional power.

(2) Iran has seen the instability in the region as a serious threat to its national security and has looked for ways to counter or contain that instability. These have ranged from active mediation in conflicts to tacit support for ex-Soviet authoritarian governments and for continuing Russian hegemony in CIS security structures.

(3) In the economic sphere the way is open for a general intensification of relations with neighbouring countries whose economies used to be oriented towards Moscow and the interrepublican trade of the Soviet Union; Iran sees potential new markets for its non-oil exports, potential supplies of raw materials for its industries, and possible partners in economic cooperation of all kinds, particularly the energy sector. The development of economic links offers special benefits to Iran's northern frontier provinces and may help to smooth out some of the unevenness in Iran's own economic development. In the

longer term Tehran has hopes for the transformation of ECO into an Islamic common market; it also sees a central geo-economic place for itself in a new transit and communications network linking the heart of the Eurasian continent with the Persian Gulf.

(4) In the realm of culture, there is the inviting prospect of resuming cultural relations with several 'Muslim' countries that were for centuries part of the same Persian Islamic cultural world as Iran. Iran sees a special role for itself in helping these countries rediscover their spiritual and cultural roots after a long estrangement under Russian and Soviet rule.

(5) Finally, an important consideration has been to maintain and develop the existing friendly and mutually beneficial relations with Russia.

How successful has Iran been in addressing these issues and achieving its objectives? On balance the record of achievement is probably satisfactory from Tehran's point of view, if not wholly positive. The development of political relations has proceeded relatively smoothly. There were significant obstacles to overcome – several of the new states were suspicious of Iran both as a revolutionary Islamic state and as a major regional power, and there was an active campaign led by Turkey and the USA to discourage the new states from developing relations with the Islamic Republic – but Iran has managed to overcome many of the suspicions and develop normal political relations with all the FSS states. The competition with Turkey for regional influence has abated without either side having gained a decisive advantage. Obstacles do remain, however, and are particularly evident in relations with Azerbaijan, which have been marked by considerable volatility, and with Uzbekistan – Islam Karimov has thawed very slowly to Iran's embrace.

Regional instability remains a source of anxiety, but fears of an uncontrollable conflagration dragging in neighbouring states have now significantly receded, and Iran has been able to minimize the impact on itself of nearby post-Soviet conflicts. Though neither the Karabagh nor the Tajikistan conflict could be described as near to resolution, they now present much less of a threat than they did in 1992–3. The reassertion of Russian security interests to the external frontiers of the FSU is a mixed blessing for Iran: a revitalized Russian superpower would be unwelcome, but the current level of Russian military presence and assertiveness is more a source of reassurance than anxiety.

Economic relations have generally developed fairly smoothly and rapidly from a very low starting-point. Trade has reached significant levels with Azerbaijan and Armenia, though largely as a consequence of the blockades that have reduced the access of those countries to CIS markets and supplies. Trade and economic cooperation with Turkmenistan have also progressed well and without the assistance of such distortions. On the multilateral level the rejuvenation and expansion of ECO and the initiation and development of Caspian Sea cooperation have been diplomatic successes for Iran and offer future prospects, even if they have produced few concrete results so far. More broadly, in the short term there are strict limitations on the possible development of economic relations with the FSS countries, because of Iran's lack of access to the investment capital required to make a significant contribution to their economic development and to build its own infrastructure to serve their transit needs.

Iran's promotion of Islamic Persian civilization as a unifying force capable of facilitating regional cooperation and stability has had limited appeal. Only in Tajikistan has there been much genuine enthusiasm for Iran as a cultural partner. In the other FSS states there are strong reservations stemming from religious, cultural, linguistic, and national differences. Nevertheless, Iran has been able to sign a number of cultural agreements and derives considerable satisfaction from the revival of Islam in the region, even if it has been denied an active role in this process. It has not been the official policy of the Islamic Republic to sponsor radical political Islamic groups in the FSS, and there is little or no convincing evidence to suggest that support for such groups is coming from Iran (either in the form of covert government backing, or from independent Islamic foundations and other agencies). If cultural relations have developed less rapidly and warmly than was anticipated, Tehran has at least achieved a cultural presence in all of the FSS states and is better placed to counter negative perceptions of Iran and to promote its own cultural and religious agenda.

If Iranian policy towards the FSS since 1989 has been broadly consistent and oriented towards the attainment of goals that have more to do with national interest than ideological commitment, this does not make it easy to predict the future development of relations, and certainly does not necessarily mean that Iran's overall commitment to radical Islamic values and causes is diminishing. While in the short term one can confidently foresee the current momentum in relations continuing, it is not difficult to imagine scenarios in which relations would take a different, if no less intensive turn.

A change in the leadership in Tehran, which must occur in 1997 when Akbar Hashemi-Rafsanjani will complete his second term as president, could lead to a significant realignment in the Iranian leadership. The consensus achieved for the current leadership's pragmatist policies may prove impossible to maintain and the possibility of a more hardline government cannot be ruled out. Such a government might have a different understanding of the correct priorities for an Islamic foreign policy in the FSS. More broadly, the success or failure of the pragmatist leadership's economic reforms will to a large extent determine the medium-term social and political stability of Iran. If they succeed, and if domestic and international investment recover, Iran could become a major regional economic force and might even be able to realize some of its geo-economic ambitions. It remains, however, extremely unlikely that

Iran will be able to attract significant international investment while its relations with the USA remain so bad. This is not the place to attempt to apportion responsibility for the breakdown in US–Iranian relations; what is clear is that the enmity is a self-indulgence that the USA can afford and Iran cannot. The inexorable logic of this situation would seem to be that ultimately Iran will have to make concessions to bring about a reconciliation, or at least normalization of relations.

Similarly, changes of leadership in the FSS countries, for instance the departure from the scene of Heydar Aliyev, could have a sudden and disruptive impact on relations. More generally, the FSS region remains politically volatile and unpredictable. In few, if any, of the states is political authority firmly consolidated or effectively legitimized. Existing unresolved conflicts may well flare up again, and there are many other sources of ethnic and socio-economic tension. The emergence of a radical Islamic mass movement is by no means inconceivable and could in certain circumstances present a serious challenge to Tehran's current prioritization of stability before support for radical Islam.

Finally, any significant change in Russian policy towards the FSS, or in Russian–Iranian relations, could significantly affect Iranian policy towards the FSS. If a nationalist expansionist Russia began to erode the independence of the FSS states and present a threat to Iranian security, then the balance of Tehran's priorities would change accordingly. If a neo-isolationist or economically incapacitated Russia decided to abandon its commitment to CIS security structures and the maintenance of the FSU's external frontiers, that also would call for a reconsideration of Iranian policy.

It is, however, always easy to think of alarming scenarios. Stepping back for a moment from Tehran's interests and objectives, it is worth attempting an assessment of Iran's record of involvement with the FSS states in terms of their own interests and objectives. On balance it is hard to avoid the conclusion that Iranian interests and policies have broadly coincided with those of the FSS states. Iran's role in the Karabagh and Tajikistan conflicts compares favourably with that of other regional powers and certainly has not fuelled the conflicts; in the case of Tajikistan it made a real contribution to achieving a cease-fire. Iran's diplomatic offensive also seems to have been broadly compatible with the FSS states' objectives of diversifying their political relations and gaining acceptance in the world community. Similarly Iran's multilateral initiatives with ECO and Caspian cooperation at least have the potential to serve a useful function in developing regional stability and economic cooperation and in bringing the Caspian states together to tackle the real and urgent issues that confront them. Iran's economic contribution has been fairly modest to date, but all the FSS states have welcomed it as a trade partner and have also expressed interest in its development as a bridge to the Persian Gulf. In the sphere of cultural relations, the fact that Iran has refrained from supporting radical Islamic groups accords with the interests of the FSS governments and the majority of their inhabitants, and the restoration of cultural relations on the basis of Persian Islamic civilization cannot be interpreted as a serious threat, though it may not be particularly appreciated. On the whole the intensification of existing relations, particularly in the economic sphere, would be beneficial for both Iran and the FSS states. Conversely, it is clear that the artificial severing of relations between Iran and its new northern neighbours would be damaging to regional stability and inimical to the political and economic interests of the latter.

SOURCES AND FURTHER READING

The principal sources used, in addition to those cited in the footnotes, are: the Foreign Broadcast Information Service, *Daily Reports* for Central Eurasia and for the Near East and South Asia; and the BBC, *Summary of World Broadcasts*, Part 1 Former USSR, and Part 4 Middle East.

The following works are suggested for further reading:

K.L. Afrasiabi, *After Khomeini: New Directions in Iran's Foreign Policy* (Boulder, CO: Westview Press, 1994)

R. Allison (ed.), *Political and Economic Challenges in Post-Soviet Central Asia and the Transcaucasus* (Washington DC: Brookings for the RIIA, forthcoming 1995).

A. Banuazizi and M. Weiner (eds), *The New Geopolitics of Central Asia and its Borderlands* (London and New York: I.B. Tauris, 1994).

J. Calabrese, *Revolutionary Horizons: Regional Foreign Policy in Post-Khomeini Iran* (Basingstoke: Macmillan, 1994).

S. Chubin, *Iran's National Security Policy: Capabilities, Intentions and Impact* (Washington DC: The Carnegie Endowment for International Peace, 1994).

A. Ehteshami (ed.), *From the Gulf to Central Asia: Players in the New Great Game* (Exeter: University of Exeter Press, 1994).

P. Ferdinand (ed.), *The New Central Asia and its Neighbours* (London: Pinter for the RIIA, 1994).

M. Haghayeghi, *Islam and Politics in Central Asia* (New York: St Martin's Press, 1995).

S. Hunter, *Iran and the World: Continuity in a Revolutionary Decade* (Bloomington, IN: Indiana University Press, 1990).

G. McDonell, *The Euro-Asian Corridor: Freight and Energy Transport for Central Asia and the Caspian Region* (London: RIIA, Post-Soviet Business Forum, 1995)

M. Mesbahi (ed.), *Central Asia and the Caucasus after the Soviet Union: Domestic and International Dynamics* (Gainesville, FL: University Press of Florida, 1994).

Y. Ro'i (ed.), *Muslim Eurasia: Conflicting Legacies* (London: Frank Cass, the Cummings Centre Series, 1995).

G. Winrow, *Turkey in Post-Soviet Central Asia* (London: RIIA, Former Soviet South Paper, 1995).

I.D. Zviagelskaia, *The Russian Policy Debate on Central Asia* (London: RIIA, Former Soviet South Paper, 1995).

In addition, the journals *Central Asian Survey* (London) and *Central Asia Monitor* (Fair Haven, VT) regularly contain articles relevant to the Former Soviet South and its international relations.